SAYS WHO?

"

Twelve Popular Christian Assumptions
Examined by Scripture

R. B. Ouellette

A previous edition of this book was published in 2006 by Sword
of the Lord Publishers under the title *Things that Aren't So.* This
updated and edited edition was first published in 2019 by Striving
Together Publications, a ministry of Lancaster Baptist Church,
Lancaster, CA 93535. Striving Together Publications is committed
to providing tried, trusted, and proven books that will further
equip local churches to carry out the Great Commission. Your
comments and suggestions are valued.

Striving Together Publications
4020 E. Lancaster Blvd.
Lancaster, CA 93535
800.201.7748

ISBN 978-1-59894-394-8
Printed in the United States of America

DEDICATION

This book is dedicated to Scott Cowling, my faithful colaborer, loyal assistant, and son in the faith. No one has worked harder to lighten my load or to hold up my hands. I love and appreciate you very much.

ACKNOWLEDGMENTS

I wish to acknowledge with gratitude the amazing work done by the team at Striving Together Publications. This is the sixth project on which we have worked together. I am, as always, impressed with the professionalism of the process and the product. Special thanks to Monica Bass, a wordsmith of amazing ability, and to Andrew Jones for his always-impressive and creative graphics.

CONTENTS

INTRODUCTION

Simple questions can make a big impact. Radical changes in human society have come about through curious minds that dared to contest popular assumptions.

Think back to 1492. What if Christopher Columbus never challenged the myth of the flat earth? America as we know it today might not exist.

Fast forward to the nineteenth century. What if doctors continued using contaminated instruments because Joseph Lister never probed the existence of bacteria in wounds? Many preventable deaths would have continued to occur.

I'm thankful for those brave pioneers who determined to confront popular assumptions and establish the facts. And if the search for truth bears great significance in the scientific world, how much more so in the spiritual realm? As Bible-believing Christians, we should be relentless in the quest for veracity, testing popular assumptions with inerrant Scripture. We should be willing to question our preconceived ideas: "Does the Bible say that, or is it just man's assumption?" When confronted with common sayings or philosophies that appear true, we should obey the admonition of 1 Thessalonians 5:21 to, "Prove all things; hold fast that which is good."

That's what this book is about. Together, you and I will examine twelve popular assumptions in the light of Scripture. We'll look into God's Word as we analyze myths, partial truths, and even lies well-meaning Christians believe.

On this journey, we'll look at questions such as, "Is burnout inevitable?," "Does God care only about the heart?," and "Is there a difference between big sins and little sins?" The assumptions behind these questions may seem insignificant, but their impact shows otherwise. For example, I've seen believers abandon God's will because they had a misconceived view of burnout. And I've watched Christians ignore outward sin in their lives because they're convinced God only looks at the inward man. I've also heard Christians excuse sin because they don't view their wrongdoing the way God does.

Some of the assumptions examined in these pages are those I've had or believed previously. I was born into a pastor's home, and the Lord is still teaching me truths from His Word. Whether you've been saved for five months, five years, or five decades, you're not immune to assumptions. I pray that, by the end of this book, you'll be challenged, convicted, and better equipped to continue in the truth of God's Word.

We'll examine each assumption through a three-fold grid:

- **The Common Teaching**—In this section, I'll present what many Christians assume to be true on the topic. I'll explain various viewpoints and even the Bible passages they have applied (in some cases, incorrectly) to reach their conclusions.

- **The Contradictory Truth**—Here we'll look at how these conclusions hold when contrasted with other Bible truth. In some cases, the original assumption may have been correct, in some, partially correct, and in others, wrong.

- **The Truth Applied**—We'll close each chapter examining how we can apply scriptural truth to our lives. After all, the purpose of truth isn't simple knowledge or debate; it is application and life change.

Join me now as we challenge popular assumptions with the unchanging truth of God's Word.

CHAPTER ONE

Is Burnout Inevitable?

Several years ago, I went to the doctor about some pain in my knees. In the eighties, I had arthroscopic surgery, but my knees were bothering me again. After visiting my doctor, he referred me to a specialist who did several tests to determine the severity of the problem.

The specialist showed me a sample X-ray. "These are the knees of a seventy-year-old man," he explained. Then he showed me the X-rays of my knees. "Yours are worse," he said. "You're ready for a knee replacement. Your knees are just worn out."

That got me thinking about the topic of burnout. It's something we often hear about today. There's a great deal of focus on the danger of falling prey to overwork and stress, and some even believe it's inevitable.

The truth is that many of us do work hard. In Christian ministry, often unseen are the 2:00 AM phone calls, late-night counseling sessions, hours of study and door knocking, and the list could continue. Burnout, however, is not the inevitable result of keeping up a hectic ministry schedule. Throughout history to present day, you'll find examples of Christian workers who have served the Lord fervently and joyfully throughout their lifetime in spite of difficult times and demanding schedules. I believe that God provides ways for us to avoid burnout and have many fruitful years of service for Him.

THE COMMON TEACHING

It is commonly taught that twenty-first-century Christians are overworked, overstressed, and in danger of burnout. Some say, "It's just *so* hard in the day that we live. We have more pressures, stress, and difficulty than we ever did before. We have to be on guard for burnout."

Proponents place a strong emphasis on rest and back up this teaching with Mark 6:31, "And he said unto them, Come ye yourselves apart into a desert place, and rest a while...." The belief is that if you don't come apart and rest, you'll come apart.

Now, I'm not against rest. I've always tried to take a day off each week and family vacations each year, and those things are important. However, I've heard people use the phrase "come apart and rest" to justify quitting regular times of witness or teaching their Sunday school class. I know there are times when God leads us to make changes in ministry, but if you are feeling so overwhelmed by your schedule and responsibilities that you feel the need to cut something out, start with the things that don't have eternal value.

While it is true that we live in a fast-paced society with unique challenges, I believe we can still learn from the example of first-century Christians. Let's take a closer look at the disciples in Mark 6: "And the apostles gathered themselves together unto Jesus, and told him all things, both what they had done, and what they had taught. And he said unto them, Come ye yourselves apart into a desert place, and rest a while: for there were many coming and going, and they had no leisure so much as to eat" (Mark 6:30–31).

Based on this verse alone, you might believe, as many do, that after a season of intense ministry, Jesus told the disciples to come apart and rest because they had already been overextended and any more ministry pressure would likely be greater than they could handle. But let's take a closer look at these verses in context to get a better understanding of what led the disciples to this point and how they managed to avoid burnout.

THE CONTRADICTORY TRUTH

The disciples were exhausted. Mark 6 reveals that Jesus had sent the disciples out two by two into the countryside to preach the gospel (verses 7–13). People responded to the message so well that the disciples didn't have time to eat because they were so busy ministering. Most of us would probably admit that eating is high on our priority list.

Jesus recognized His disciples' exhaustion and took them to a desert place. Mark 6:32 says, "And they departed into a desert place by ship privately." They needed some time away. But as the story continues, we find that the people followed the ship on foot when they saw Jesus leaving. "And the people saw them departing, and many knew him, and ran afoot thither out of all cities, and outwent them, and came together unto him" (Mark 6:33).

Can you picture this passage coming to life? When the people saw Jesus and the disciples leaving, they didn't just casually stroll towards the boat, hoping they'd catch Him. They *ran* out of the city. We sometimes overlook the tremendous appeal Jesus had to the common people. They would literally follow Him everywhere He went. If I were in the disciples' sandals and saw a swarm of people rushing toward the boat, my spirits probably would have sunk.

The Sea of Galilee is eight miles wide and thirteen miles long. In the day of Christ, there were nine townships on its shores with no less than fifteen thousand people living in them. As those who saw Jesus and the disciples leaving followed along the shoreline, people from the adjoining cities joined them so they could also hear Jesus.

When Jesus got off the boat, the Bible says He "saw much people." I think, based on the fact that we are told there were five thousand men, that it's reasonable to assume there were twenty thousand or more people there to hear Him.

Instead of sending the crowd away, Jesus welcomed them. This next verse offers an incredible glimpse into the heart of our Saviour: "And Jesus, when he came out, saw much people, and was moved with compassion toward them, because they were as sheep not having a shepherd: and he began to teach them many things" (Mark 6:34).

Instead of trying to get away from these people, Jesus was moved with compassion. What a comforting thought that God never wearily pushes me away when I come to Him for instruction. He wants to teach me, just as He wanted to teach the multitude. He sees us with compassion, eagerly waiting to help us with our problems, shortcomings, and questions.

Time passed as the people sat spellbound under the voice of the Master. Finally, the disciples reached the end of their patience. They came to Jesus, saying, "This is a desert place, and now the time is far passed: Send them away...for they have nothing to eat" (Mark 6:35–36).

But the Lord had a different plan. He told the disciples, "give ye them to eat." After this statement, I can imagine the disciples looking at each other, confused. They had no food to give them—what was He talking about?

Jesus asked, "How many loaves have ye? go and see." He wasn't focused on what the disciples lacked; He wanted to know what they did have.

In our lives, it's easy to complain about how we lack the time or energy to accomplish a task. The next time you're tempted to dwell on your lack of resources, ask God to multiply what you do have. Don't give up. If the disciples had given up because they were tired or discouraged, they would have missed out on an amazing miracle. And I have to wonder, how many blessings and miracles do we miss out on because we give up?

The disciples gathered five loaves and two fish from a young boy and gave them to Jesus. Jesus then instructed the disciples to divide the crowd into groups, and serve the food, which he multiplied. If our estimate of 20,000 people in the crowd is correct, each disciple would have needed to distribute food to around 1,700 people. The day that had been devoted to resting was devoted to ministry instead.

After everyone had eaten their fill, the disciples gathered what was left over. The Bible tells us there were twelve baskets of food left over—one for each of the disciples but none for Jesus. Jesus did not use His divine power for personal benefit. Instead, He chose to refresh His strength in prayer.

At His urging, the disciples left Jesus and travelled across the lake. Mark tells us, "And straightway he constrained his disciples to get into the ship, and to go to the other side before unto Bethsaida, while he sent away the people. And when he had sent them away, he departed into a mountain to pray" (Mark 6:45–46).

Jesus was as tired physically as the disciples, if not more so. He undoubtedly needed a day of rest as much as they did. All day long He had taught the multitude who gathered to hear Him. He had performed a miracle, something that exacted a physical toll on Jesus (Mark 5:30).

Yet rather than taking the night to sleep, Jesus chose to pray. He knew that for the coming days, He would need strength that was not His own. While sleep is important, physical rest alone will not sufficiently strengthen us for the spiritual battles we face. If we try to do things in our own strength, we will burn out. We need God's power working in and through us, and the only way to obtain that kind of supernatural strength is to spend time in His presence.

While Jesus was praying, the disciples were sailing calmly on the Sea of Galilee until suddenly, a massive storm arose. The fearful disciples began frantically bailing water out of the side of the boat, just trying to stay above the waves.

Jesus, in His omniscience, knew that His disciples needed His help. He wasn't going to leave them stranded to battle the waves on their own, and He began walking toward them on the sea. Mark 6:48 says, "And he saw them toiling in rowing; for the wind was contrary unto them: and about the fourth watch of the night he cometh unto them, walking upon the sea, and would have passed by them."

Imagine the fear of the disciples when they saw a shadowy figure approaching them on the water. "What's that?" the disciples must have cried. But the figure called out, "Be of good cheer: it is I; be not afraid." It was Jesus! When Jesus came into the ship, the storm ceased. Mark 6:51 says, "And he went up unto them into the ship; and the wind ceased: and they were sore amazed in themselves beyond measure, and wondered."

The Bible says Jesus came to the disciples around the fourth watch—sometime close to morning. The disciples had engaged in hard physical work all night, and they must have been exhausted. Surely after getting back to shore, they settled down for some much-needed, deserved rest and woke up refreshed and ready to tackle the week of ministry ahead. Right? Well, not exactly.

After a long day of no rest, followed by a night of no sleep, a terrifying storm, and hard work bailing water, the disciples started all over again the next day. Read Mark 6:54–56 carefully. Nothing indicates that they rested. "And when they were come out of the ship, straightway they knew him, And ran through that whole region round about, and began to carry about in beds those that were sick, where they heard he was. And whithersoever he entered, into villages, or cities, or country, they laid the sick in the streets, and besought him that they might touch if it were but the border of his garment: and as many as touched him were made whole."

Not only did the disciples not get extra rest that day, but they also got no rest. As soon as they got to shore, the cycle of ministry started again. In the passage (Mark 6:30–31) often cited as an example to quit on our responsibilities to rest, we see that the disciples, in fact, did not get any rest. Stopping to rest was the original plan, but it didn't work out that way. And yet, the disciples didn't burn out—not that day, not ever. We watch each of them (with the exception of Judas Iscariot) continue to live fruitful lives for the Lord, literally turning the world upside down with the message of Jesus Christ.

You may think, "That's great. The disciples didn't burn out. But how did they do it? More importantly, how do I avoid burnout?" Having a biblical approach to this question can sometimes determine whether or not someone continues to serve God. Together, let's look at practical, biblical steps we can take to avoid burnout.

THE TRUTH APPLIED

If we were to make a list of busy people in the Bible, the Apostle Paul would rank high on that list. Through his testimony, we'll see the first key to avoiding burnout.

Rely on the grace of God. Below, we read a description of just a part of Paul's life.

> Are they ministers of Christ? (I speak as a fool) I am more; in labours more abundant, in stripes above measure, in prisons more frequent, in deaths oft....in perils by the heathen, in perils in the city, in perils in the wilderness, in perils in the sea, in perils among false brethren; In weariness and painfulness, in watchings often, in hunger and thirst, in fastings often, in cold and nakedness. Beside those things that are without, that which cometh upon me daily, the care of all the churches.—2 CORINTHIANS 11:23–28

What an incredible testimony! Paul survived stoning, spent twenty-four hours floating in the ocean, was constantly in danger, thrown in jail, beaten, verbally abused, and traveled extensively—all while writing much of the New Testament. If anyone needed a vacation, surely it was Paul.

But in spite of everything he had been through, not only did Paul continue to serve faithfully, but he also encouraged other Christians to serve God with their whole hearts just as he did. Through his preaching and ministering, he left a powerful impact on the world for Jesus Christ.

What was his secret? Paul didn't rely on his own strength; he relied on God's grace, and that mentality shaped his ministry into the dynamic, powerful testimony we remember it as today.

Even at our weakest, God can give us grace to serve Him. But what is grace in our Christian lives? Fundamentally, grace is a supernatural enabling to serve, obey, and live for God. Paul had a thorn in his flesh. He asked God three times to remove it, but God said no: "And he said unto me, My grace is sufficient for thee: for my strength is made perfect in weakness. Most gladly therefore will I rather glory in my infirmities, that the power of Christ may rest upon me" (2 Corinthians 12:9).

God's grace is sufficient—it is everything you could possibly need. Sometimes, we don't feel like we have the energy to do our work, and until we realize that we cannot do things in our own power, we'll continue to struggle with these feelings of insufficiency. We cannot do God's work without God's power.

The Lord didn't say, "*Your* strength is made perfect in weakness." He said, "*My* strength is made perfect in weakness." When we recognize that we are weak without the Lord and turn to Him for strength, He'll give us everything we need. In fact, it is in our weakest moments that we experience God's strength the most. He delights in taking our insufficiencies and working through them. God will never give us something that we cannot handle with His strength.

Allow God to renew you. Remember Elijah in the Old Testament? He was a courageous, fiery preacher who was mightily used of God. But he struggled with exhaustion and discouragement. He reached a point where he wanted God to take his life:

> But he himself went a day's journey into the wilderness, and came and sat down under a juniper tree: and he requested for himself that he might die; and said, It is enough; now, O Lord, take away my life; for I am not better than my fathers. (1 Kings 19:4)

But God didn't reply, "Elijah, get up and get going. There's work to be done."

Instead, God responded with gentle care: "And the angel of the Lord came again the second time, and touched him, and said, Arise and eat; because the journey is too great for thee" (1 Kings 19:7).

As humans, we have our physical limits, and Elijah had reached his. God doesn't expect us to run on two hours of sleep and eight cups of coffee every day. When we get discouraged and weary like Elijah did, God isn't a cruel taskmaster who doesn't care or understand. He wants to give us the strength and replenishing that we need to continue serving Him joyfully.

When Elijah was at his weakest, God provided for his physical needs and gave him divine strength for the journey ahead. Elijah went on to do incredible things for the Lord. God's strength is key to avoiding burnout. His grace is always sufficient for our needs.

Recommit yourself to praising the Lord instead of worrying. One of the most basic and foundational truths we all need to grasp is that God created us to work. In the Garden of Eden, before sin entered the world, Adam and Eve didn't just lounge around. They were actively busy. Work isn't a result of sin; it's something we were created to do. Look at Ephesians 2:10: "For we are his workmanship, created in Christ Jesus unto good works, which God hath before ordained that we should walk in them."

We were "created in Christ Jesus unto good works." God has an exciting plan that He wants each of us to accomplish. When we find God's will and pursue it with all of our hearts, we can find joy and rest in the One who has ordained our steps even when trouble comes.

Many Christians are so overwhelmed by all that they have to do that they lose their joy. If we would replace griping and worrying with praying and praising, we'd have peace instead of stress. It takes a lot of energy to worry and complain.

The Bible tells us, "Be careful for nothing; but in every thing by prayer and supplication with thanksgiving let your requests be made known unto God" (Philippians 4:6).

Did you catch that? When we replace worry with prayer and thanksgiving, God gives us peace. When Jesus instructed the disciples to feed the multitude, their first reaction wasn't, "Okay, Lord, we don't have a lot, but we're ready to do what you've instructed. We're ready to watch You work a miracle." Their first reaction was to look at what they lacked. Like the disciples, we tend to focus on our shortcomings instead of relying on God. We forget that it takes a lot of energy to get upset—energy that we could channel into accomplishing the task at hand.

God tells us to come to Him in prayer rather than allow our lives to be filled with worry. There is no problem too large or too difficult for God. When we make the decision to surrender our worries, fears, and problems to the Lord, we will find our strength and energy renewed.

Take care of your physical and spiritual health. Even in our busiest times, it's important to care for our bodies. Your body is the temple of the Holy Spirit (1 Corinthians 6:19), and it deserves proper care and attention. It is the physical instrument you use to serve God.

The great Scottish preacher, Robert Murray McCheyne, was mightily used by God to spread revival across Scotland. His journal had a great impact on the life of the missionary David Brainerd. Yet McCheyne was so eager to work that he neglected his health. He died before he was thirty years old. On his deathbed, he told a friend, "God gave me a message to deliver and a horse to ride. I have killed the horse and can no longer deliver a message."

Rest is important. In fact, God set the standard for rest when He rested on the seventh day of creation. God created our bodies to need rest.

Living a healthy lifestyle is also important. Try to exercise throughout the week. Get the sleep that you need. Visit the doctor for regular physical checkups. Eat a nutritious diet including fruits and vegetables. Exercise and a healthy diet fuel our bodies to perform at our peak. I eat better now than I once did. I go to the salad bar at restaurants. Sometimes, I even eat broccoli on purpose. I have learned that as I take care of my body, I'm able to serve the Lord more effectively.

Although physical health is important, your spiritual health needs to be your prime concern. First Timothy 4:8 says, "For bodily exercise profiteth little: but godliness is profitable unto all things, having promise of the life that now is, and of that which is to come." What's on the inside—in your spirit—affects what's on the outside—your body.

Sin harbored in the heart harms the body (Psalm 32:1–4). This is why it's vital that we ensure our spirit is right with God. Pray with thanksgiving. Think on things that are good, pure, lovely, honest, and just (Philippians 4:8). Our outlook is determined by what we meditate on.

Burnout is not caused by overworking the flesh; it is caused by overworking *in* the flesh. We can accomplish incredible things for the Lord, but if we are fueled by our own strength, we'll eventually burn out.

What would happen if you ran your car's motor without oil? Eventually, you'd ruin your engine. And that's what happens when you run your body without the Holy Spirit. You wear out. As believers, we have something that many of the busiest executives in our nation don't— we have God's infinite power, grace, and strength at our disposal. If we rely on Christ and truly discover that His grace is sufficient, we do not have to burn out, no matter how difficult life's challenges get.

God gives us an amazing promise in Isaiah 40:28–31:

> Hast thou not known? hast thou not heard, that the everlasting God, the Lord, the Creator of the ends of the earth, fainteth not, neither is weary? there is no searching of his understanding. He giveth power to the faint; and to them that have no might he increaseth strength. Even the youths shall faint and be weary, and the young men shall utterly fall: But they that wait upon the Lord shall renew their strength; they shall mount up with wings as eagles; they shall run, and not be weary; and they shall walk, and not faint.—ISAIAH 40:28–31

When God gives us a purpose to fulfill, He also gives us the strength to fulfill it. Wait upon the Lord. Ask Him for strength. God delights in showing Himself strong in your life.

CHAPTER TWO

Were the Men in Acts 6 Actually Deacons?

A jewelry store owner was making some last-minute preparations before she went on vacation. She had a line of jewelry that wasn't selling well and told her staff to cut the price in half. When she returned, she was simultaneously shocked and delighted. Not only had every piece sold, she received double the original price. Her staff had misread her note and thought that the jewelry's price was supposed to be doubled, not cut in half. When people noticed the dramatic price increase, they automatically assumed the jewelry valuable, and they wanted to buy it.

What we believe influences our behavior. The customers in that jewelry store purchased the over-priced jewelry because they assumed it was more valuable than it actually was. Similarly, what we assume about the Bible impacts our actions.

THE COMMON TEACHING

A common teaching among Christians is that the men in Acts 6 were the first deacons and that their actions should be the model for our deacons today. Embedded in this assumption is the possibility of an unbiblical view of church government that could hinder the body life of the church. To get the story, let's look at Acts 6:

> And in those days, when the number of the disciples was multiplied, there arose a murmuring of the Grecians against the Hebrews, because their widows were neglected in the daily ministration. Then the twelve called the multitude of the disciples unto them, and said, It is not reason that we should leave the word of God, and serve tables. Wherefore, brethren, look ye out among you seven men of honest report, full of the Holy Ghost and wisdom, whom we may appoint over this business. But we will give ourselves continually to prayer, and to the ministry of the word. And the saying pleased the whole multitude: and they chose Stephen, a man full of faith and of the Holy Ghost, and Philip, and Prochorus, and Nicanor, and Timon, and Parmenas, and Nicolas a proselyte of Antioch.—ACTS 6:1–5

The Grecians and the Hebrews were having a disagreement over their widows being neglected. The apostles developed a plan and had seven godly men selected to care for the widows and serve the church.

Many godly Christians believe that these seven men were the first deacons. For example, John R. Rice wrote in the Rice Reference Bible, "These seven men, we suppose, were the first deacons. Note first that they were servants of the church. *Deacon* is the Anglicized Greek word for *servant*. These men were to care for poor widows in the church."

If you believe similarly, as many of my friends in ministry do, my goal isn't to attack your belief, but to challenge your thinking. The technical name and role for the seven men in Acts 6, while important, is a smaller part of the big picture. The larger issue I want to explore is to what extent this passage prescribes the functioning aspects of church government.

Many believe that if the men in Acts 6—Stephen, Philip, Prochorus, Nicano, Timon, Parmenas and Nicolas—were the first deacons, the duties and responsibilities they had should set the pattern for the work of deacons today. They explain their teaching like this:

The Greek word *diakonos* is used to describe these men. If you look back to our passage, you won't find the word *deacon* mentioned. The underlying Greek word that describes the men's work, however, is *diakonos*. *Deacon* is simply the Anglicized form of the Greek word that we use today to describe this office within the church. Many good commentaries explain that this is the reason we don't actually have the word *deacon* in the text.

Although commentaries are helpful and they can greatly support your study, they aren't inspired. I never forgot a lesson my Bible college professor, Dr. Rupp, taught me. He said, "Before you go to commentaries, read the Bible. After you get everything you can out of the Bible, then go to the commentaries." He explained that using commentaries with little Scripture is one way that errors creep into the church.

"Suppose someone writes a good commentary, but gets one principle wrong," Dr. Rupp said. "The overall commentary is good, and it becomes widely used. In the next generation, someone else decides to write a new commentary and uses the old one because it's so widely accepted. They repeat the error because they trust the old commentary. And slowly, the wrong interpretation of Scripture gets passed down from generation to generation."

Don't get me wrong—I believe in study. My library is filled with tools that I use to prepare sermons and lessons, but I never want to treat them as the final authority in place of the Word of God.

The deacons were chosen to handle the business matters of the church while the disciples handled the spiritual matters. The disciples said, "Wherefore, brethren, look ye out among you seven men of honest report, full of the Holy Ghost and wisdom, *whom we may appoint over this business*" (Acts 6:3).

Many take that instance and assume that the deacons' job was to handle the business matters of the church while the disciples' job was to handle only the spiritual matters. After all, the disciples said that they would handle the spiritual matter, telling the church, "But we will give ourselves continually to prayer, and to the ministry of the word" (Acts 6:4).

This distinction does not mean, however, that the disciples relinquished responsibility of interest in the management of the church. They couldn't physically accomplish everything that needed to be done and selected men to handle one responsibility—taking food to the widows of the church.

The deacons are to care for the business of the church and allow the pastor to care for the spiritual concerns. When a church creates a responsibility divide between the pastor handling the spiritual matters and the deacons handling the administrative matters, the deacons may begin to assume an unbiblical level of authority. In this scenario, the pastor may then step away from his God-given role of leadership and leave the deacons to make decisions in which he actually should provide leadership for the flock.

For example, I knew of a church that practiced this way. The pastor would "hide" behind his deacons anytime a policy came up that was controversial. When the issue arose about remarrying people who had been previously divorced, the deacons met to discuss it. After much deliberation, they issued a policy that said, "The pastor is directed not to perform weddings where one of the parties has been divorced."

The pastor's lack of involvement bothered me. Finally, I asked him why he personally didn't step out and say what he believed. He told me, "It's harder for people to get mad at eight men than it is for them to get mad at me."

Unfortunately, his attitude reflects what many pastors feel. If he can just let the deacons take responsibility for the tough issues, he doesn't have to get involved.

I've learned that when deacons or committees take that kind of responsibility, the pastor will have a difficult time exercising effective leadership in the church.

Even if the men in Acts 6 were the first deacons, that still would not serve as a pattern for such a decision of responsibility within the church.

The only task we know of that those seven men had was to take food to the widows each day. They were appointed to that task by the disciples. There is nothing in Scripture to suggest that these men had any responsibility or authority in other church business.

I once heard about a couple who had been married thirty years and promised that they had never fought once. Finally, someone asked them what their secret was. The husband replied, "We agreed when we got married that I would make the big decisions and she would make the small decisions. In thirty years of marriage, we've never had a big decision, so there's never been anything to fight about!"

You'll find that husband's attitude in many churches. The line between spiritual matters and administrative matters gets blurred, and the deacons assume more and more responsibility to the point that the pastor exercises very little leadership at all.

Years ago the deacon chairman of a church contacted me. His church was looking for a pastor, and he asked if I thought my dad would be interested in the job.

I replied, "He might; but if my dad comes, he will be the pastor."

The deacon responded, "Absolutely, we believe that. We want the pastor to lead the church. Of course, the deacons are going to watch him and make sure he doesn't do anything we don't think he should do." The deacon failed to recognize what the biblical roles of the pastor and deacon are.

Of course, when pastors do wrong, there are biblical guidelines for dealing with sin or errant doctrine. A church family shouldn't be critically watching their pastor because they want to "catch" him, but neither should they blindly assume that he is incapable of doing wrong.

A man in our church didn't like something I announced I was going to preach and asked our deacons if they thought it was right for me to preach on that topic. They told him, "We don't make those decisions. Talk to Pastor."

There is no biblical model for deacons dictating spiritual business or decisions of the church.

THE CONTRADICTORY TRUTH

We've looked at the view some hold that the men in Acts 6 were deacons and at the potential ramifications of that view. I'd like to share why I believe the Bible teaches these men were godly men, but not the first deacons. As we unpack this truth, keep the big picture in mind of how this relates to biblical church leadership.

There are three problems with believing that the first deacons were found in Acts 6:

The men in Acts 6 are never called deacons. *Diakonos* is used throughout the passage, but in different ways. In verse 1, it is translated *ministration*. In verse 2, it is translated *serve*. In verse 4, it is used in the phrase *the ministry of the word*. A basic definition for *diakonos* is "to serve." Throughout the Bible, it is used to describe a servant.

The use of this same word in verse 4 is critical to understanding the passage. It describes, not the work of the seven men serving food to the widows, but the work of the apostles in preaching and teaching the Bible. The apostles, not the seven men, said, "But we will give ourselves continually to prayer, and *to the ministry of the word.*"

We cannot conclude just from the Greek word used that the seven men chosen in Acts 6 were deacons. If we did, we would have to believe that the apostles were deacons as well, since *diakonos* is used to describe their actions.

The Bible word *diakonos* is used many times in Scripture where it could not be referring to deacons. *Diakonos* does sometimes refer to a deacon, but not always. For example, Luke 10:40 says, "Martha was cumbered about much serving"; but no one would argue that the use of the word *diakonos* to describe her makes her a deacon. Luke 17:8 uses the same word: "Make ready wherewith I may sup, and gird thyself, and serve me." The house servant putting the meal on the table was certainly not a deacon in the church.

The requirements for deacons in 1 Timothy 3 are different from the requirements in Acts 6. First Timothy 3 describes both the requirements for the pastor and the deacons. The qualification of Acts 6:3 was that the men be "of honest report, full of the Holy Ghost and wisdom." But the list in 1 Timothy is different:

> Likewise must the deacons be grave, not doubletongued, not given to much wine, not greedy of filthy lucre; Holding the mystery of the faith in a pure conscience. And let these also first be proved; then let them use the office of a deacon, being found blameless. Even so must their wives be grave, not slanderers, sober, faithful in all things. Let the deacons be the husbands of one

wife, ruling their children and their own houses well.
—1 TIMOTHY 3:8–12

If the men in Acts 6 were deacons, why wouldn't there be at least one or two overlapping qualifications? I believe the omission is because 1 Timothy 3 and Acts 6 are speaking of different positions.

The pastor, not the deacons, is to take care of the church. The pastor is to provide oversight for the church. Let's take a closer look at how that plays out in New Testament churches.

If you look at the qualifications for church offices given in 1 Timothy 3, you will find many parallels between the pastor and the deacons. Each is required to be blameless, the husband of one wife, to rule his house well, to not struggle with alcohol, and to not be motivated by greed.

But look at what is said about the pastor in verse 5: "For if a man know not how to rule his own house, how shall he take care of the church of God?" (1 Timothy 3:5). Nowhere in Scripture is this said about the deacons. God places the responsibility of leadership, the "care of the church of God," on the shoulders of the pastor. The same Greek word is used in Luke 10:35 when the Good Samaritan told the innkeeper, "Take care of him." According to *Vine's Expository Dictionary,* the word indicates foresight, provision, and focusing on the needs of others.

Simply put, God holds the pastor accountable for both the spiritual and administrative well-being of the church and its members (Hebrews 13:17). Since he will answer to God, he needs to take responsibility for the decisions that are made and the direction of the church.

There is no place in the New Testament where a deacon ever makes a decision for a church. I'm thankful for the deacons at our church, and I count these dedicated men as good friends. They care deeply about our church and about the Lord. Their contribution as deacons, however, lies in their service, not in their leadership. That's the pattern established in Scripture.

Although I value the advice and input of these men, God holds me, as the pastor, ultimately responsible for the First Baptist Church of Bridgeport. I'm the leader of the church, not because I desire power, but because that is the way God intended for the church to function.

THE TRUTH APPLIED

Looking at the history and proper role of deacons leads us to these conclusions:

Tradition does not equal truth. If we're not careful, we can twist tradition in our minds to become equal to Scriptural truth. It's easy to fall into the mindset of "we've always done it that way." I'm all for traditions—our church and my family have them. But that doesn't make them biblical commands that can never be broken. For example, we usually have a candlelight service at our church every

Christmas Eve. But if we didn't have it one year, we wouldn't be doing anything wrong.

When I first started pastoring our church, I learned that the church had elected many officers—from a Sunday school superintendent to a treasurer to a church clerk. While there is nothing wrong with this model, there also is no biblical basis for these elections—the Bible only teaches two offices in the church. At First Baptist of Bridgeport, then, we discontinued the practice.

The problem with tradition is that it becomes so ingrained in our minds that we accept something that may be contrary to God's Word as truth. Jesus said, "But ye say, Whosoever shall say to his father or his mother, It is a gift, by whatsoever thou mightest be profited by me; And honour not his father or his mother, he shall be free. Thus have ye made the commandment of God of none effect by your tradition" (Matthew 15:5–6).

Practice is not always based on principle. A man had been married only a month. The first time his new wife fixed a pot roast, he watched in amazement as she sliced off both ends before putting it into the pot.

"How come you're cutting off the ends?" he asked.

"My mother always did it that way," she replied.

After some discussion, they called her mother and asked why she cut off the ends of the roast before cooking it. "When we first got married," she said, "I had a pot that was too little to put a whole pot roast in. So I'd trim off both ends to make it fit!"

You may not be cutting off the end of a pot roast to get it to fit in your Crock-Pot, but many of us have traditions that, on closer inspection, just don't make sense.

When I was a student in college, the women were allowed to iron clothes in their dorm rooms, but the guys were not. One of the young men asked why this rule was in place. After some investigation, he found out that the electrical current in some of the old men's dorms was not sufficient for all of the appliances. Though the problem with the electricity had been corrected years earlier, the rule was still in place. There was no principle involved in the rule, so there was no problem changing the rule once it was brought to the attention of the authorities.

These examples remind us that it's so important to be careful that our practices are based on a principle and not because "I've always done it this way, so it must be right."

Widespread unscriptural practices can occur when we accept as gospel things that aren't so. A few years ago, a preacher friend of mine left a church he had started and went to pastor another church. The new church had about sixty people when he got there. He was faithful to preach and emphasize soulwinning, and the church began to grow.

One day he was sitting in his office when one of the deacons came in. The deacon said, "You may be the pastor of this church, but I'm the manager." The pastor had his Bible on his desk. He picked it up and said, "That's interesting. I've read this several times, and I've never found that. Would you show it to me, please?" The deacon couldn't find it, but he still thought he should be the manager of the church.

That deacon is hardly alone in his belief—but he is wrong. The pastor is the leader of the church, and many problems arise when we substitute tradition for what Scripture says. We have generations of Christians who have bought into the false concept that the deacons are responsible for the business of the church rather than the pastor.

Based on my understanding of Acts 6, I don't believe that those men were the first deacons. But I look at that as the small picture. The big picture I want you to take away is the biblical view of church leadership. If you're a pastor, rest confidently in the truth that God has given you a role of authority. It's a grave responsibility, but it's not something to shy away from. If you're a deacon, support and love your pastor. Do what you can to encourage him in his role as the leader and help him however you're able. And if you're a church member, support your pastor and pray for him as he seeks to be the biblical leader God called him to be.

CHAPTER THREE

Is a Wife Always Responsible to Obey Her Husband?

Submission.

When it comes to the husband/wife relationship, it's incredible how many Christians are divided over one word—*submit*. Should the wife submit to her husband? How much should she submit? Should she *always* submit? What if her husband asks her to do something that contradicts God's Word? Should she still obey her husband, or should she obey God?

The short answer is that biblically, wives should submit to their husbands. The Bible clearly states this command: "Wives, submit yourselves unto your own husbands, as unto the Lord" (Ephesians 5:22).

But the Bible also gives a larger, more nuanced answer to this challenging question. In some difficult situations, we need to understand the fuller answer. Take for example a counseling situation I had years ago.

A woman in our church came to me for help with her marriage, and my heart hurt for her as she told her story. Her sincere but misguided belief in absolute submission had tragically altered her life. Her backslidden husband had pressured her into his sinful lifestyle. At first, he required that she go with him to the bar. Later, he forced her to drink with him. His demands grew even worse, including requests for her to break their marriage vows, and she continued to go against her biblical convictions because she felt like she had no choice but to obey her husband completely.

She looked at me with tears in her eyes and said, "I was taught I should always obey my husband. I didn't know what else to do." Her heart was broken, not just because of her husband's actions, but because of the devastation she had suffered by going against her conscience.

Many Christians (including myself for many years) believe that a wife should obey her husband without exception. But as I encountered situations like this one, I began to take a closer look at Scripture. Slowly, I discovered that this idea of no-exceptions submission is not only unbiblical, but it can cause great harm to a godly Christian wife.

Understanding what the Bible says about submission in marriage is crucial. First, for those of us who are or will be married, a scriptural view of the role between the husband and the wife helps us deepen our relationship with our spouse. Second, a biblical outlook helps us navigate tough, real-life situations that demand biblical answers.

THE COMMON TEACHING

God has ordained the husband to be the head of the home and the wife to be in submission to her husband. "Wives, submit yourselves unto your own husbands, as it is fit in the Lord" (Colossians 3:18). The first two words in that verse—wives, submit—don't leave room for argument. God is clear in His view on the wife's role in her marriage. But those who believe in no-exceptions submission misunderstand the scope of verses like Colossians 3:18. To back up their view, they make three points.

There is no exception clause to submission in Scripture. God does not say, "Submit to your husbands... unless he's unreasonable."

He doesn't command, "Submit to your husbands...but use your discretion."

He doesn't tell us, "Submit to your husbands...unless he asks you to sin or do something you're uncomfortable with."

He says, "Wives, submit."

Because they believe the Bible is silent on what to do when a husband asks his wife to sin, many say that we don't have the liberty to make exceptions.

The wife is under an umbrella of protection. If we don't have the liberty to make exceptions, then there must be some sort of umbrella of protection for the wife. Her husband's authority is an umbrella of protection over her, and the husband will ultimately answer to God for any sin in which he as the leader made his wife participate.

There are indeed areas over which a wife has no control, and God will not hold her accountable for her husband's actions. For example, an unsaved husband may be the sole source of income in the home, but he refuses to tithe on the money he earns. The wife cannot make her husband tithe, and she will not answer to God for his not tithing.

Although the umbrella of protection may be a helpful analogy when describing the importance of submission to one's authorities, it doesn't provide an excuse to disobey the Bible. God's command to obey earthly authority doesn't automatically mean our command to obey God becomes secondary. Remember, one day we will stand before God and give an account for ourselves (Romans 14:12). When that happens, the husband is not going to stand by his wife, taking responsibility for sin he asked her to commit.

The wife cannot use the excuse of obedience to God for disobedience to her husband. Those who believe in no-exceptions submission would come to the conclusion that because the wife is under an umbrella of protection, she can't use the excuse of obedience to God for disobedience to her husband. God said for a wife to submit to her husband, and that settles it in their minds. No exceptions. No special cases. Just submit. Furthermore, they say that if a wife is doing her best to be a good wife, it's likely that her husband will never ask her to do something wrong in the first place.

On paper, this interpretation of the verse sounds legitimate. But in real life, it's a little more complicated. How do you respond when a heart-broken woman comes to you like the woman I mentioned earlier?

Some people answer, "She was obviously not doing all she could to be the right kind of wife. Otherwise, her husband would have never required her to do *that*."

Inadvertently or not, statements like those blame the victim. A wife holds great influence on her husband, but he alone is responsible for his actions. Even if the wife isn't doing all she can to be a godly wife, her husband's actions are not her fault. More than that, those statements ignore the principle of personal accountability. The wife is always responsible for her actions, just as the husband is always responsible for his.

Maybe you don't place the blame on the wife at all, but you struggle with excusing such a seemingly straightforward command—"Wives, submit." Furthermore, there are other commands in the Bible that we sometimes don't fully understand or that can be difficult to follow, so why would we make an exception for this one?

I do believe that sometimes God asks us to obey Him in hard areas or to follow Him in faith even when we don't understand. But obeying God in the hard areas will never require us to go against one of His commands. And I don't believe we are excusing this command by choosing to study it in light of other passages.

THE CONTRADICTORY TRUTH

To help us better understand what a wife's submission should look like toward her husband, let's start by looking at a different authority relationship—the relationship between a Christian and the government.

God's command for Christians to obey the government is as clear and direct as His command for wives to obey their husbands. There is no room for doubt in the words to the following verses:

> Let every soul be subject unto the higher powers. For there is no power but of God: the powers that be are ordained of God. Whosoever therefore resisteth the power, resisteth the ordinance of God: and they that resist shall receive to themselves damnation. For rulers are not a terror to good works, but to the evil. Wilt thou then not be afraid of the power? do that which is good, and thou shalt have praise of the same: For he is the minister of God to thee for good. But if thou do that

which is evil, be afraid; for he beareth not the sword in vain: for he is the minister of God, a revenger to execute wrath upon him that doeth evil. Wherefore ye must needs be subject, not only for wrath, but also for conscience sake.—ROMANS 13:1–5

Whether the government is good or bad, moral or immoral, peaceful or violent, we are to submit. Think about the government that was in place when Paul wrote Romans 13. Nero, the emperor of Rome, was one of the most corrupt rulers in history. He burned Christians on poles to light his gardens at night for his parties. Yet Paul, under the direct inspiration of the Holy Spirit, wrote that Roman believers should obey the authority of Nero because he was "ordained of God."

That's a heavy command. Imagine being a Christian during the rule of a sadistic man like Nero. I can almost picture the Christians saying, "Paul, are you sure we're talking about the same government here? Nero isn't exactly neutral toward our beliefs. Surely you don't mean that we have to obey him. He's actively seeking to kill us." But yes, Paul was asking believers to submit to Nero. In light of Nero's reign, it's sobering to consider the magnitude of what Romans 13 is asking. Submission to authority, any authority, is a big deal to God.

With that in mind, compare the clarity of the passage on a wife's submission to her husband with the clarity of the passage before.

> Wives, submit yourselves unto your own husbands, as
> unto the Lord. For the husband is the head of the wife,
> even as Christ is the head of the church: and he is the
> saviour of the body. Therefore as the church is subject
> unto Christ, so let the wives be to their own husbands
> in every thing.—EPHESIANS 5:22–24

Wives have an obligation to obey their husbands, just as Christians have an obligation to obey their government. Though the relationship is different, the principle of the Christian's obedience to the government is no different from the wife's obedience to her husband. We are to submit.

But this brings up an interesting point—something that will help us understand the extent of our submission to authority. What happens when the government orders us to do something against God? For example, what if we're told that we can't say certain sins are wrong because we'd be engaging in hate speech? Or what if we're told we can no longer freely share our faith? Does God still want us to submit? Do we submit to authority, even when asked to go against God?

Through a specific incident in Peter's life, we see the answer. In Acts 5, the council forbade the apostles from preaching in Jesus' name. Although the Roman governor was the ultimate authority, the governor delegated to the Jewish religious leaders (the council) the power to govern religious matters in an attempt to keep the peace.

The apostles were called to answer to the council for why they continued to preach in Jesus' name. The accusations against the men were flying. Didn't they know that it was illegal for them to preach the gospel? Peter wasn't shaken and boldly responded, "… We ought to obey God rather than men" (Acts 5:29). Let that courageous statement sink in.

We ought to obey God rather than men.

Rather than councils commanding us to stop sharing our faith.

Rather than kings asking us to eat the king's meat and wine (Daniel 1:8).

Rather than laws requiring the murder of babies for population control (Exodus 1:16).

Rather than husbands demanding that we go against the Bible.

This verse doesn't just apply to Peter and the other apostles. This is a principle that applies to every human authority, whether it be the government or your husband. The command to obey is not absolute if the authority issues a clear mandate that goes against God.

In some instances, the Bible notes and commends those who *disobey* government in order to obey Him. The same Apostle Paul who was inspired by the Holy Spirit to write, "Let every soul be subject unto the higher powers" was also imprisoned for willfully disobeying the government. He, like Peter, continued preaching when he had been told to stop.

We don't just have examples about submission to government authority in Scripture. God also shares with us examples of wives both submitting and not submitting to their husbands. Let's look at two of these examples. When each were confronted with the decision to obey either God or man, they chose two different paths, and the outcome for each woman was drastically different.

Abigail's response—Abigail is an example of a wife who rightly went against her husband's wishes. The Bible describes her husband Nabal as being "churlish and evil in his doings" (1 Samuel 25:3). Abigail, in contrast, is described in the same verse as "a woman of good understanding, and of a beautiful countenance."

King Saul was out to kill David, and David was fleeing for his life. While he was in hiding, he met Nabal—not exactly your friendly next-door neighbor as we'll soon see—who lived near one of his hiding places. David treated Nabal well. David and his men didn't steal any of Nabal's sheep (a common practice of soldiers in David's day), and he even protected Nabal's workers for weeks. Now, David needed some basic provisions. He wasn't asking for much, and considering what he and his men had done, it was the least Nabal could do. But to David's indignation, Nabal not only refused, but also thoroughly insulted him.

David and his men were livid. In retaliation, they prepared to go to battle against Nabal. When Abigail heard the news, she knew that Nabal and his sheepherders had no chance of survival against David and his men of war. Without telling her husband, she determined to do all she could to prevent fighting and prepared a peace offering that she personally took to David. She didn't just bring David a little bread and some water; she went above and beyond. "Then Abigail made haste, and took two hundred loaves, and two bottles of wine, and five sheep ready dressed, and five measures of parched corn, and an hundred clusters of raisins, and two hundred cakes of figs..." (1 Samuel 25:18).

Abigail personally begged for David's forgiveness for her husband's rash behavior. Although she knew her husband was against her actions, she knew his pride and folly were about to get everyone in the house killed.

In response to Abigail's passionate plea for mercy, David agreed to not attack Nabal's household. But because of Nabal's wickedness, God killed Nabal. And, in a unique plot twist, Abigail ultimately married David.

The point is this: nowhere do we see the Bible condemning Abigail's actions for going against her husband Nabal. She was potentially preventing bloodshed, doing all that was in her power to keep the peace, and paving the way to reconciliation.

Likewise, there are times when a wife may be in a similar situation to Abigail. And during those times, the wife has a higher calling to obey her Lord.

Achan's wife's response—Abigail's obedience resulted in a happy ending. But in the story of Achan's wife, the story ends differently. In Joshua 6:18-19, God commanded the Israelites not to take the spoil from the destruction of Jericho. But when Achan, one of the soldiers, walked through the city, he saw treasures that he wanted. In direct contradiction to God's instructions, he took some of the spoil.

When Achan returned home with his newfound wealth, his wife decided to be complicit in his actions . The consequences were disastrous:

> So Joshua sent messengers, and they ran unto the tent; and, behold, it was hid in his tent, and the silver under it. And they took them out of the midst of the tent, and brought them unto Joshua, and unto all the children of Israel, and laid them out before the Lord. And Joshua, and all Israel with him, took Achan the son of Zerah, and the silver, and the garment, and the wedge of gold, and his sons, and his daughters, and his oxen, and his asses, and his sheep, and his tent, and all that he had: and they brought them unto the valley of Achor. And Joshua said, Why hast thou troubled us? the Lord shall trouble thee this day. And all Israel stoned him with stones, and burned them with fire, after they had stoned them with stones.—JOSHUA 7:22–25

Maybe you've read the story of Achan before and thought, "Wow, that's a harsh punishment for Achan, let alone for his family." He, his wife, his children, and even his animals were stoned.

But remember where Joshua's men discovered Achan's stolen goods? In his tent, indicating that Achan's wife and children (likely already adults) were accessories after the fact to his theft. Even though Achan's wife and children weren't responsible for Achan's theft, they were complicit in helping him continue in it.

Achan's wife and children were under Achan's protective umbrella of authority, but they were not excused for tolerating sin. They were responsible for their actions and were not exempted from punishment.

The same way that God held Achan's wife responsible for her sin applies to the wife's submission to her husband's authority. In everything they can, wives should submit. They may not agree to their husband's idea, but as long as it's not sinful, they should support him. However, the moment a husband asks his wife to do something that is biblically wrong and she still does it, she is responsible to God for her actions.

A situation like the one I described above is not God's intention for marriage. Just as the wife is commanded to submit, the husband is commanded to love his wife. A spirit-filled husband never acts like a tyrant, commanding his wife to do things against her will just because he can. He will listen to her preferences. He will respect her opinions. And he will not ask her to do something that goes against her conscience. In a biblical marriage, the husband leads while the wife influences. Their roles are equally important, and the marriage is not a dictatorship—it's teamwork.

THE TRUTH APPLIED

In our imperfect world, not all marriages follow the biblical patterns outlined in Scriptures. So if a husband asks that a wife do something that goes against God, how should she respond?

Right now, you may be in the middle of a tough marriage. Your husband is asking you to do things that deeply go against your core biblical beliefs. But after reading these pages, you're starting to see that you should not submit to your husband when doing so goes against God's Word. Still, you're not sure how to proceed. How do you biblically honor God and your husband at the same time? Here are three guiding principles:

Keep a good attitude. Although Paul refused to obey authority, he still kept a submissive attitude. He was bold, but he remained Christ-like. He spoke the truth, but he spoke it in love. He didn't compromise his convictions, but he wasn't antagonistic.

When I think of the apostle Paul, I don't think of an angry man shouting at the top of his lungs. I don't see him bashing the government and deliberately stirring contention. Although Paul did not have control over the consequences of his actions, he did have control over his attitude. He remained firm in what he believed while peacefully submitting to the consequences of his actions.

Like Paul, you need to keep a kind and submissive attitude. If you're in a position where you need to go against your husband's unbiblical wishes, ask the Lord to help you have that same meek attitude. (Of course, if you're in an abusive situation, you should seek immediate help and protection. Never stay in a situation that is physically unsafe.)

Part of having the right attitude is having the right heart behind your submission to God over authority. We should never respond with a knee-jerk reaction to a requirement we don't necessarily like. It's vital that our decision to disobey authority in order to obey God is firmly founded in Scripture. Sometimes, good men can be deceived into believing something that the Bible doesn't teach. I remember a pastor who encouraged his church to rebel against the government's authority. He refused to pay employment taxes for church employees and suggested that his members not get involved with the government. Because of that man's decision, the church was sold off to pay taxes they never should have owed. We need to be careful not to fall into the trap of going our own way and justifying it by saying that we're obeying God. When you come to a place where you need to submit to God over your husband, do so with discernment. Have a clear biblical basis for your position.

God gives us clear examples of men and women who went against the government to obey God. While they were respectful and submitted to the consequences of their actions, they recognized that God's authority must be final.

Realize that God's authority is the highest standard. Long before Paul, we see a story of the Hebrew midwives who chose to obey God rather than man. Pharaoh, worried about the growing number of Hebrews in his kingdom, commanded the midwives to kill all newborn baby boys. By doing so, he hoped to institute a means of population control.

Because the midwives feared God (Exodus 1:17), they refused to obey Pharaoh's wicked command. In fact, when they were called to account for their disobedience, they lied about what they had done. Far from condemning their decision to disobey, the Bible records, "Therefore God dealt well with the midwives: and the people multiplied, and waxed very mighty. And it came to pass, because the midwives feared God, that he made them houses" (Exodus 1:20–21).

Made them houses is a Hebrew idiom, meaning that God rewarded the midwives for their disobedience to the government by giving them families of their own. God rewarded the midwives' obedience to Him even when it required disobedience to Pharaoh.

No authority—whether an Egyptian Pharaoh, government official, pastor, or husband—has the right to tell anyone to disobey God. Human authority is always below God's authority.

For example, our church supports missionaries in China who are completely "underground." They attempt to keep their mission work out of sight because the government would persecute them if their actions were detected. They've correctly realized that to obey the government would require breaking God's command to fulfill the Great Commission.

In America, we have the privilege of freely sharing our faith. But that may not always be the case. If witnessing becomes illegal, we should respectfully disagree, continue to share our faith, and accept and submit to the consequences of obeying God rather than man.

It's the same for a wife. God's authority is always her highest standard. Not only is it permissible, but it is also biblical for her to obey God above what her husband says.

Look for ways to please God and your husband. Even if you're in a tough situation, ask God for grace to help you find ways to please your husband. You may not be able to do everything that he asks because of your obedience to God. But try to honor your husband in areas you can, down to the small, preferential ones. Often, when a wife is stubborn and angry, an unsaved husband will retaliate by pressuring his wife to go against her conscience.

Get to know your husband's preferences and try to meet them. Let him know that you support him in every area that you can and that you love him unconditionally. If you're working to please and honor your husband, it can have a powerful impact on his attitude and behavior toward you.

If you have experienced a marriage situation like the one I've been describing, I'm so sorry. I pray that your husband will one day have the same relationship with the Lord that you do.

Meanwhile, if your husband asks you to do something that goes against God, rest assured—we are never asked to do something that expressly goes against Scripture. There is never a circumstance where disobeying the Lord is justified. God's authority is always the highest authority.

Never give up hope that God can change your husband's heart. Your response to your husband is hugely instrumental in that. God says, "Likewise, ye wives, be in subjection to your own husbands; that, if any obey not the word, they also may without the word be won by the conversation of the wives; While they behold your chaste conversation coupled with fear" (1 Peter 3:1–2).

Your actions as a godly wife have a powerful impact on your unsaved husband. You could be influential in bringing him to the Lord. God is a miracle-working God, and there is no marriage too difficult for Him to transform.

CHAPTER FOUR

Will God Pour Out Unbelievable Blessings if We Tithe?

According to an old story, someone asked John D. Rockefeller, the world's first billionaire, how much money it would take to satisfy him.

His reply? "A few dollars more."

Many of us wonder how someone as wealthy and successful as John D. Rockefeller—someone who, in the world's eyes, has arrived—could be discontent with what he had. But if we stop and think more closely, doesn't his attitude reflect that of many in our world?

Something about money seems to affect us more than anything else. Many Americans work fifty to sixty hours a week just to earn "a few dollars more." Turn on the news and you'll hear about thefts, murders, embezzling, immorality, and drug sales that are all committed in the pursuit of money. Money is an obsession for many in our society.

Unfortunately, even some Christians allow money to become an idol in their lives. This desire for wealth can influence teaching in churches today. Perhaps you've heard or believed that God promises unbelievable blessing if we obey Him in our tithes. But is that true? Or are we interpreting verses like Malachi 3:10 incorrectly?

THE COMMON TEACHING

God says in Malachi 3:10, "Bring ye all the tithes into the storehouse, that there may be meat in mine house, and prove me now herewith, saith the Lord of hosts, if I will not open you the windows of heaven, and pour you out a blessing, that there shall not be room enough to receive it."

Many read this verse and think, "There it is! This verse clearly states that God will bless those who tithe beyond their ability to receive." At first glance, this teaching is exactly what Malachi 3:10 says. If we faithfully tithe, God will give us so much that we won't be able to handle it all.

I once asked our church members, "How many of you have ever prayed, 'Lord, I can't take any more blessing. I've got money in every bank in town that exceeds the Federal Deposit Insurance Corporation insurance. Lord, please, no more. I've had more blessings than I can receive'?" No one said yes.

But wait a minute. Doesn't God *promise* to give us amazing blessings if we tithe? If we're not experiencing an abundance of money, does that mean that we're not tithing properly? Or does the problem lie in our understanding of the verse?

It's likely that you could identify with the members of our church—you're probably not experiencing overabundant, more-than-you-can-receive blessing because you tithe.

Those who adhere to this common teaching respond to this potential issue by saying that this verse isn't referring to material blessings, but to a "window" of special wisdom and insight, since tangible things don't usually come through windows. For example, if you tithe, you'll understand how to become a better worker, parent, or spouse. They teach that Malachi 3:10 is metaphorical—it's not actually saying that God will give you material blessing as a reward for tithing.

The bottom line of the teaching is that, whether financial or spiritual, God promises to give amazing blessings to those who tithe. But let's dig a little deeper into what God says about tithing. Although blessings do come with obedience, I think we easily misinterpret this verse.

THE CONTRADICTORY TRUTH

It appears that we're being told showers of abundant blessing come our way if we tithe. But as we take a closer look, we'll see this isn't the case. Notice these reasons:

Tithing isn't optional; it's a clear command from God. Scripture tells us that you can't be right with God and not tithe. Leviticus 27:30 says, "And all the tithe of the land, whether of the seed of the land, or of the fruit of the tree, is the LORD's: it is holy unto the LORD."

The tithe belongs to God. When you keep it, you're stealing from God. In fact, it is holy unto God, meaning that it is sanctified, or set apart. It belongs especially to Him.

Some believe that, while we should give, tithing is actually an Old Testament doctrine. Because we're not under the law, the command of tithing no longer applies to us. I'd challenge this, however. Four hundred years *before* the Law was given to Moses, Abraham paid tithe to Melchizedek (Genesis 14:17–20). Furthermore, Jacob promised to tithe when he saw his vision of the angels of God at Bethel (Genesis 28:10–22). Although God included tithing when He gave Moses the Law (Leviticus 27:30; Numbers 18:24–26; Deuteronomy 12:6), it was not a new practice.

Jesus didn't see tithing as optional. He told the Pharisees, "Woe unto you, scribes and Pharisees, hypocrites! *for ye pay tithe* of mint and anise and cummin, and have omitted the weightier matters of the law, judgment, mercy, and faith: these ought ye to have done, and not to leave the other undone" (Matthew 23:23). Jesus didn't condemn the Pharisees for tithing; He *commended* them for tithing. You'd have to look hard for areas where Jesus approved of the Pharisee's behavior, but this was one of them. Although the Pharisees were wrong in many areas, they were right in being careful to tithe, even on the herbs that they grew.

Tithing is an eternal principle. It was practiced before the Law, commanded under the Law, and commended by Jesus who came to fulfill the Law.

But why does the God who owns everything really need our money—the money He even gave us in the first place? A big reason why God commands us to tithe is that He wants to establish in our minds His ownership of everything. He wants us to learn to fear Him properly. Deuteronomy 14:22-23 speaks of this: "Thou shalt truly tithe all the increase of thy seed, that the field bringeth forth year by year. And thou shalt eat before the LORD thy God, in the place which he shall choose to place his name there, the tithe of thy corn, of thy wine, and of thine oil, and the firstlings of thy herds and of thy flocks; that thou mayest learn to fear the LORD thy God always."

What would happen if someone got up in your church and prayed this honest prayer before the offering: "Dear Heavenly Father, thank You for giving us the opportunity to give back a portion of what You have given us. I pray that You would bless those who obey and judge the crooks."

That prayer wouldn't be politically correct, but it would be scripturally correct. God calls those who don't tithe thieves. Malachi 3:8 says, "Will a man rob God? Yet ye have robbed me. But ye say, Wherein have we robbed thee? In tithes and offerings." By not tithing, we're robbing God.

A pastor friend of mine once told me about a special offering night his church had years ago. There was a boy there without his parents, and they had to stop him from taking money *out* of the plate as it went by. Apparently, he didn't quite get the concept of an offering!

We smile at this story, but perhaps we do the same thing in a more sophisticated way. If you were low on gas and knew you weren't going to get paid until Friday, you wouldn't dream of taking a little out when the offering plate came by like that little boy did. But there is no difference in God's eyes between taking money out of the offering plate and failing to put our money into the plate.

The tithe doesn't become the Lord's once it goes into the offering plate; it already belongs to Him. When you receive money into your possession, you become a steward of God's money, and He has designated 10 percent of that money to be given to the local church. It has always been His money, and it is no less stealing to leave it in your bank account than it is to take it out of the offering plate.

Malachi 3 was addressed to the nation of Israel, not individuals. Most of the commandments God gave His children had a definite enforcement mechanism to provide punishment if they were violated. Tithing is one of only a handful of commands with no human enforcement system set up under the law.

God takes the matter of giving so seriously that He enforces the punishment Himself. That is what God did to Israel in Malachi 3:9. God said, "Ye are cursed with a curse: for ye have robbed me, even this whole nation." Taken in context, this verse is key to understanding Malachi 3:10. Both verses are referring to the entire nation of Israel.

There is a *principle* for individuals in this passage, but the promised blessing is for the nation. God said He would pour out a blessing if "ye" bring the tithes. *Ye* is a plural pronoun. It is not used for an individual. If the promise were for individuals, the language would be "Bring thou" the tithes. This passage was never intended to be an individual promise.

As we study the Bible, one of the easiest mistakes we make is taking what God says out of context. To truly understand what the Lord is teaching us, we have to take the whole passage in the way that God wants us to interpret it.

When it comes to understanding verses in the Bible, while they should be taken literally, we can't simply rely on the open-and-point method. I heard about a man who was praying for God's direction in his life and tried this method with disastrous results. The first verse he found said, "[Judas] went and hanged himself" (Matthew 27:5). He didn't think that was what God was saying, so he opened his Bible again. The second verse he found said, "Go, and do thou likewise" (Luke 10:37). He thought he'd give it one more try, but the third verse he opened to said, "That thou doest, do quickly" (John 13:27).

That man was having some serious issues with taking verses out of context. He was looking at the Bible as some sort of magical device. He failed to realize that we're commanded to read and study God's Word systematically and contextually. In 2 Timothy 2:15, Paul said, "Study to shew thyself approved unto God, a workman that needeth not to be ashamed, rightly dividing the word of truth."

The words translated *rightly divided* in our English Bible carry the idea of "cutting straight." Picture yourself installing hardwood floors in your house. If the wooden pieces aren't cut straight, it will be impossible to lay the pieces together correctly. In the same way, we need to be sure that we use God's Word carefully, letting it mean everything God intended but not reading our preconceptions into it. Otherwise, we'll be putting our own twist on Scripture, making it say something God never intended for it to say.

Years ago, there was a pastor not too far from our church who preached an entire sermon from the phrase in Jeremiah 23:28, "The prophet that hath a dream, let him tell a dream." He told his people about the dreams he had for the church and how he wanted the church to grow and change and move ahead.

I appreciate the pastor's heart to dream big for God, but that pastor did not "rightly divide" this passage to his people. The next phrase in the same verse says, "…and he that hath my word, let him speak my word faithfully." The whole point God is making in that verse is that a person's dreams don't carry weight like His Word does. In fact, later in the verse, God compares our dreams to chaff and His Word to wheat. While the pastor's sermon was motivating, it wasn't biblical.

Context is key. When you study the Bible, ask yourself, "To whom is God speaking? What is He saying to them? What does He say before and after it? How does that apply to my life?" Only as we do that can we rightly divide God's Word. As we apply the context to the promise in Malachi 3, we see that God was addressing the nation of Israel rather than individuals.

God makes a clear distinction between tithing and giving. As we've already seen, the tithe belongs to God (Leviticus 27:30, 32). When I tithe, I am fulfilling an obligation to the Lord. I'm simply paying Him something that I owe Him. In all the years we've lived in our home, I've never once received a thank-you note from the mortgage company for making a house payment. Why not? Because I owed that payment to the bank.

If you let someone borrow your car to run an errand, you don't thank him for giving you a car when he brings it back. It's no big deal to return to someone what already belongs to him. Likewise, God owes us nothing for giving the tithe back to Him because it belongs to Him.

I believe that you are blessed by God for tithing because it is an act of obedience just as you are blessed for reading the Bible, faithfully going to church, praying, obeying your parents, and sharing the gospel.

The greater blessing is for those who go beyond the tithe and also give offerings. Proverbs 3:9–10 tells us, "Honour the Lord with thy substance, and with the firstfruits of all thine increase. So shall thy barns be filled with plenty, and thy presses shall burst out with new wine."

While tithing alone may not bring greater blessing beyond the general blessing of obedience, God promises to fully provide for our needs as we give generously to Him. Paul emphasized this promise when he wrote to the sacrificially giving church at Philippi, "But my God shall supply all your need according to his riches in glory by Christ Jesus" (Philippians 4:19).

THE TRUTH APPLIED

By now, you may be thinking, "I get that Malachi 3:10 doesn't mean I'm going to be the next millionaire when I tithe. But the Bible still does promise abundant blessing. If that blessing is not promised to me personally, where does it go?"

I believe the answer is that the local church as a whole receives the blessing. This answer is consistent with the principle that two are better than one.

Two can always accomplish more than one can alone. For example, in some areas of our country, there are contests called horse pulls to measure the strength of horses. Two horses together can pull an average of twenty times greater weight than one horse can pull alone. The Bible teaches this as well.

Leviticus 26:8 says, "And five of you shall chase an hundred, and an hundred of you shall put ten thousand to flight: and your enemies shall fall before you by the sword." The verse is saying that if five chase a hundred, the ratio is 1 to 20. When one hundred put ten thousand to flight, the ratio is 1 to 100. Five people together have power, but one hundred people together have much greater power. This is the same principle taught in Malachi 3.

God multiplies blessing when His people join together in His work. In general, if you double the number of people doing the work, you more than double the blessing of God.

If we could get everyone in a church tithing, the blessings would be multiplied to such an extent that there would be no way to contain them. You may be familiar with what's called the 80-20 rule. In a normal church, 80 percent of the money is given by 20 percent of the people. Typically, the work that is done follows the same pattern. The minority of the people often accomplish much more than the majority. If everyone gave, we would have no idea what to do with the money. That's the blessing God is talking about in Malachi 3:10.

Imagine what would happen for the Lord if we all gave. I think missionaries would spend less time on deputation and get to the field sooner. I think we could fund new ministries to reach people for Christ. We could print more Bibles and brochures with the gospel. We could help new churches pay for their buildings so they don't start with an overwhelming burden of debt. Giving to the Lord's work is one of the most fulfilling things we can do.

I have a preacher-friend in Ohio who started a mission church across town from his church. They bought some property and a small building, but the new church never really took off. After a few years, the area where the building was located experienced a commercial boom. Since the mission church wasn't able to sustain itself, the parent church sold the property for about $200,000 more than they had paid for it.

The church faced a decision about what to do with the money. Although there were a number of choices they could have made, they decided that since they had bought the church with missions money, they would use all the proceeds for missions. The pastor took all the missionary letters they had received from the missionaries they supported. Together, the church met the needs and requests of their missionaries.

The pastor told me that it was one of the most fulfilling times he's ever had in the ministry. The church had more satisfaction meeting the missionaries' needs than they would have had doing anything for themselves.

Imagine how wonderful it would be to do something like that all the time! If everybody tithed, that overabundance of blessing would happen.

When you don't tithe, you're not just robbing God or leaving God's work without the resources you would have contributed. You're also robbing everyone of the multiplied blessing that could come if everyone would tithe. When God's people collectively obey His command to tithe, the windows of Heaven open. Then, we have incredible resources to do great things for the Lord.

CHAPTER FIVE

Must a Pastor Leave the Ministry If His Adult Children Fall into Sin?

My dad was a pastor, and ministry has been a big part of my life since I was born. I have a special place in my heart for kids who grow up in a pastor's home, and I can relate to many of the specific challenges and pressures they face.

Ministry is awesome, but it's not always easy. When you're in the ministry, you can feel like you're living in a fishbowl. Members of the church and the community watch what you and your family do closely. Often, you feel that they hold you to a higher standard than others.

Every pastor's home is different, but if you grow up in one, you are likely in church every time the doors open.

You learn the truth of Scripture and the consequences of sin, and can recite the Romans road in your sleep. Biblical principles are ingrained in you.

Unfortunately, some pastors' children still fall into sin despite knowing the truth. Billy Sunday's son is an example. Billy Sunday traveled across America, turning cities upside down with his dynamic message. He wasn't a pastor, but he was a powerful evangelist and one of the best-known preachers of his day.

Sunday was famous for preaching against the dangers of alcohol. This message was personal to him—Sunday himself had been a heavy drinker before his salvation. His sermon "Get on the Water Wagon" was one that he preached again and again. Despite his passionate preaching against alcohol, his youngest son Paul was an alcoholic for much of his life.

After hearing stories like this, we're left shaking our heads. Why would a child who was raised with God's Word suddenly abandon ship?

There are no clear-cut reasons we could apply to every rebellious pastor's child. We could think of stories in which two children grew up in the same home but went completely different directions once they reached adulthood. Parents can do all they can to raise their children to love and serve God, but no amount of training on the parents' part can negate the principle of personal accountability. Ultimately, the choice to follow or forsake the Lord is a personal one.

If a pastor's child sins, does it disqualify the pastor from the ministry? Some would say yes, and here is why.

THE COMMON TEACHING

When a child leaves the Lord, it is heartbreaking. Whether you're in the ministry or not, you want your children to follow God. But when a pastor's adult child is living in sin, determining the next step can get complicated. Many Christians believe that if a pastor's child lives a sinful lifestyle, the pastor must, under all circumstances, resign from the ministry. This common teaching generally follows this train of thought:

The Bible requires a pastor to rule his own house well. In 1 Timothy 3 the qualifications for a pastor are listed, and included among them is that they must rule their house well.

> This is a true saying, if a man desire the office of a bishop, he desireth a good work. A bishop then must be blameless, the husband of one wife, vigilant, sober, of good behaviour, given to hospitality, apt to teach; Not given to wine, no striker, not greedy of filthy lucre; but patient, not a brawler, not covetous; **One that ruleth well his own house, having his children in subjection with all gravity; (For if a man know not how to rule his own house, how shall he take care of the church of God?)**—1 Timothy 3:1–5

There is no question that being a good husband and father is one of the requirements for pastors that Paul gave to Timothy by the inspiration of the Holy Spirit. And I don't know of any other profession that has the stipulations found in the last part of that passage. For a pastor, having obedient children is a job requirement.

The Bible teaches that proper training will produce properly behaved children. The Bible is anything but silent on how to raise our children. It's replete with examples, stories, truths, principles, commands, and encouragement. A parenting verse we quote often is Proverbs 22:6: "Train up a child in the way he should go: and when he is old, he will not depart from it." Based on this verse (and many others), our parenting does make a difference in the hearts of our children. When parents commit themselves to biblical parenting, they will have an incredible impact on the way their children behave, both when they are children and when they become adults.

When a child strays, it is always due to a failure on the part of the parents, which demonstrates negligence on the part of the pastor. Proverbs 22:6 promises that if we train our children in the way they should go, they will turn out right. But when they do not, we assume that the parents must have failed in their parenting. According to this view, it is always the parents' fault. The culmination of this thought process is that if a pastor's child goes astray, the pastor has forfeited the right to lead a church because he has demonstrated that he cannot lead his own household as required by the Word of God.

THE CONTRADICTORY TRUTH

Without question, a pastor has a definite mandate from God to rear his children properly. But in truth, God does not expect less from any other Christian parent, although the consequences for failure to do so are greater for a pastor. No matter our vocation, each of us has a responsibility to "bring them [our children] up in the nurture and admonition of the Lord" (Ephesians 6:4).

Parents have a great responsibility for their children's behavior. To an extent, we are responsible for our children's behavior, which reflects on us as parents. Think about it. When you're grocery shopping and you see a five-year-old throw a fit in the middle of the bread aisle, you probably see it as a reflection on the parents, even subconsciously. Their screaming child's behavior says something about their parenting.

We can see an even more serious example in Genesis 34. Here, we meet Jacob and his daughter Dinah. Dinah visited some ungodly friends and met a young man who forced himself on her. Then, this man asked Jacob for Dinah's hand in marriage.

Jacob's sons were outraged at how their sister Dinah was treated. They insisted that the men of Shechem be circumcised before they would allow the marriage to take place. Three days later, when the men were in pain from the procedure, Simeon and Levi, who were Jacob's sons and Dinah's brothers, killed them.

But our story doesn't stop there: "And Jacob said to Simeon and Levi, Ye have troubled me to make me to stink among the inhabitants of the land" (Genesis 34:30). The actions of two of Jacob's sons had a definite impact on his reputation. He knew that he would be held responsible for his children's deceitful behavior. Although Simeon and Levi had made a personal choice to retaliate against the men of Shechem, their actions reflected on Jacob, and he knew the people would view him as responsible for his sons' actions.

Not only do our children's actions reflect on us, but our actions also influence our children. Later in Scripture, we meet Eli, the high priest of Israel, and Samuel, a young boy who lived and worked in the tabernacle. God came to Samuel and told him that He was going to judge Eli for not restraining the behavior of his wicked sons: "And the Lord said to Samuel, Behold, I will do a thing in Israel, at which both the ears of every one that heareth it shall tingle" (1 Samuel 3:11).

God kept His word, and his judgment on Eli and his family is found in 1 Samuel 4:18. "And it came to pass, when he made mention of the ark of God, that he fell from off the seat backward by the side of the gate, and his neck brake, and he died: for he was an old man, and heavy. And he had judged Israel forty years."

The Scripture says that Eli was heavy. I think it gives us an insight into the actions of Eli's sons. Eli's obesity wasn't common in his day. For the most part, those who lived during Eli's time led an active lifestyle and ate healthily. There were no all-you-can-eat buffets, and Snickers bars hadn't been invented yet. In Bible times, you had to be a glutton to get heavy.

The priests, such as Eli, were allowed to eat part of the sacrifices that the people brought to the tabernacle. Before the office of king was created in Israel, they probably ate better than anyone else. We can make a safe assumption that Eli indulged his flesh, but he did it in a socially acceptable manner.

I've never heard of anyone leaving the pulpit because he gained too much weight. In the list of sins that we hear preached, gluttony is probably at the bottom of the list (or not even there).

If we downplay Eli's sin, we'd be appalled at the sins of his sons. 1 Samuel 2:22 says, "Now Eli was very old, and heard all that his sons did unto all Israel; and how they lay with the women that assembled at the door of the tabernacle of the congregation." Eli committed a seemingly small sin, and his sons noticed. They saw their father's lack of moderation and felt that they had the liberty to do whatever they wanted. The saying is often true that what we do in moderation, our children will do in excess.

The example you set goes far toward determining how your children and even your grandchildren will behave. The Bible repeatedly says that the sins of the fathers are visited on the children to the third and fourth generations (Exodus 20:5; Numbers 14:18; Deuteronomy 5:9). Children do not pay for their parents' sins—the verse doesn't say that the *penalty* of the father's sin is visited on them. Rather, the sins themselves are visited on them. In other words, children are likely to struggle with the same sin that the parents do. Although Eli's sons were engaging in generational sin, they were still accountable for their actions. Generational sin is powerful, but it's not an excuse for us to continue in sin. God can and will give you the power to get victory.

We also observe in Abraham's life the effect of children imitating the sins of their parents. When Abraham went to the land of Gerar, he lied about his wife Sarah, saying that she was only his sister. Sarah was a beautiful woman, and he feared the people would kill him so they could have her. He rationalized this lie because Sarah was his half-sister. Years later, when a famine arose, Isaac followed his father's footsteps back to Gerar (Genesis 26). Out of fear, he too lied about his wife. Rebekah was Isaac's cousin several times removed—technically related, but still, his lie was more blatant than Abraham's lie.

Then we come to the third generation. Jacob was notorious for his deceptive behavior. He lied about his birthright and ultimately had to flee for his life from his furious brother Esau. The pattern of sinful behavior was not only repeated from one generation to the next but it also became worse in the succeeding generations.

Whether or not you're a pastor, it's vital to model godly behavior in your life. Tolerating "small" sins like Abraham and Eli did is dangerous. When we do that, our children are likely to follow on a larger scale.

We do influence our children's actions, and we'll be held accountable for how we raised them. We are not, however, responsible for their actions.

Ultimately, adult children are responsible for their own actions. One day, all of us will answer to God for how we lived our lives—for the choices we made and the actions we took. Romans 14:12 says, "So then every one of us shall give account of himself to God." When we stand before God, blaming our parents for our behavior will have no validity.

It's so easy to get a "victim mentality," especially when society preaches that everything and everyone else is to blame but yourself. If you face struggles in life that you can't seem to break free of, there must have been something in your past that forced you into these metaphorical chains—parents, bullies, the church. But before God, those excuses don't add up.

Years ago, I remember watching a portion of The Phil Donahue Show. His guest was Dr. Stanton Samenow, a clinical psychologist with a specialty in working with criminals. He authored the book *Inside the Criminal Mind*. As I watched the interview, I grew fascinated.

Phil Donahue was almost turning purple because of what Dr. Samenow was saying. Dr. Samenow believed that people commit crimes because of the way they think. He even quoted Proverbs 23:7: "For as he thinketh in his heart, so is he."

Phil Donahue disagreed. He insisted that people commit crimes because of the way they were brought up or disadvantages in their background.

Dr. Samenow said, "I'd be glad to believe that; but in my studies I found two children from the same family, who grew up in the same neighborhood, went to the same schools, and had the same friends. One is an accountant, and the other is in jail. You never change the way people behave until you change the way they think."

Dr. Samenow was exactly right in his view of personal responsibility. Parents can do all they can to raise their children to love and serve God, but they cannot control their children's actions. Parents are responsible for their parenting; children are responsible for what they do (or don't do) with it.

If you deal with sin biblically, you rule your house well. Eli was judged but not because of his sons' behavior.

Eli was judged because he failed to respond correctly. We're told, "For I have told him that I will judge his house for ever for the iniquity which he knoweth; because his sons made themselves vile, and he restrained them not" (1 Samuel 3:13). God judged Eli, removing him from the office of priest, not because his sons were vile, but because he failed to do anything about it—to restrain them. If Eli had done what was right and his sons had still done wrong, God would have judged only them.

Eli's story reveals that it is never the sin of the child that disqualifies the leader. It is the leader's improper response. A pastor who hides the sin of a child instead of dealing with it does not meet the biblical qualification of 1 Timothy 3. (I've even heard of pastors taking their daughters to abortion clinics rather than admitting that their daughters had done wrong. They wouldn't be disqualified because of their daughter's sin, but because of how they responded to it.)

If you're a pastor with young children, how you train them is important. Encourage them to do right and lovingly correct them when they do wrong. If, on the other hand, you have older children who are leaving the truths you've taught them, don't let the devil convince you that you're unfit for the ministry. Ask the Lord to help you take the right steps to deal with the sin in your family.

By now, you may be wondering, "Is there a way to help my children continue following God, even after they become adults? As a parent in the ministry, how do I encourage my children to serve the Lord?"

THE TRUTH APPLIED

If you are a parent in the ministry, you face some unique challenges, but it is possible to have a wonderful ministry and a wonderful family. Below are a few helpful lessons that I've learned.

Rely on the Lord. Truly, the most important thing you can do is make your relationship with God a central part of your life. Psalm 127:1–3 tells us, "Except the Lord build the house, they labour in vain that build it: except the Lord keep the city, the watchman waketh but in vain. It is vain for you to rise up early, to sit up late, to eat the bread of sorrows: for so he giveth his beloved sleep. Lo, children are an heritage of the Lord: and the fruit of the womb is his reward."

Pray for your children. Teach them what is right. Rely on the Lord for His help and wisdom. Recognize the grave importance of raising your children to follow God.

I talked to a man once who had six well-behaved children. I asked, "What do you do?" He responded, "I run scared all the time." He was thankful for the way his children behaved, but he also knew that parenting was something he needed to constantly work at.

My married daughters both love the Lord. But I know something could happen tomorrow that could change that. I don't expect that to happen, but I don't live like it never could. I still pray for my daughters' hearts every day.

Create balance between ministry and family. Some say that you can either have a great family and not such a great ministry or a great ministry and not such a great family.

I remember one pastor who told me that. He picked ministry over family, and his choice negatively impacted his children. The idea that you can have one but not the other is not right. God wants you to succeed in ministry *and* parenting, and He'll help you do both. You do not have to sacrifice your children in order to have an effective ministry.

In fact, I think it's wrong for a pastor to neglect his children for the ministry. Pastors may not spend as much time at home as they would like to due to the demands of ministry, but they can still make their children a top priority. That's something I strove to do as a parent. I made mistakes, but my daughters will tell you that they never felt neglected. They never told me, "Dad, I hate it that you're gone so much." I know that they missed me, and I missed them, but I worked to be accessible and to make sure that they knew how important they were to me. I still have a great relationship with them.

Sometimes pastors say, "I would love to spend more time with my family. In fact, I know that I need to. I just feel so overwhelmed with the amount of work that I have to do."

Finding balance is tough, but you can ask the Lord for discernment in what to leave in your schedule and what to take out. Dr. Bob Jones, Sr., used to say, "Duties never conflict." We might face choices between things that compete to claim our attention, but God doesn't give impossible commands. We can do all that God commands us to.

Win your child's heart. This verse convicts me as a parent: "My son, give me thine heart, and let thine eyes observe my ways" (Proverbs 23:26). Many children in ministry homes leave the Lord, not because they have too many rules, but because their parents never won their hearts. These children saw that their parents didn't have a genuinely strong relationship with God and/or with each other. Rules are important, but without an effective relationship, they don't produce long-term results.

Watch your attitude around your children. If you don't have a servant's heart toward ministry, your children will immediately pick up on that. They need to know that being in the ministry is wonderful. You have an important part in helping them catch that spirit.

I'm so thankful that I grew up in a pastor's home. I truly believe that pastor's children have special opportunities. I loved growing up in the ministry and try to encourage pastors' children in that wherever I go.

I got that spirit from my dad. He had a heart for the Lord's work. In the early 1970s, my dad preached for a church in Detroit, Michigan. They gave him a $1,000 love offering. That's generous today, but back in those days, it was an enormous gift. My dad was very appreciative of the money. I said, "Wow, Dad. Keep that up and pretty soon you'll be in the big time." Without hesitating, he looked at me and said, "Son, I've been in the big time for twenty years."

Before the advent of cell phones and FaceTime, my dad would sometimes be gone for weeks. I missed him, but I never doubted he loved me, loved the Lord, and loved the work of the Lord. He made something positive out of everything that happened. He took time to make us feel special, and he didn't complain. My dad never pretended to be a perfect father, but I had his heart, and he had mine.

Love your children back to God. There are times when a pastor's child falls into such sin that the pastor should resign in order to give proper care to the restoration of his child and family. Sometimes, a pastor does get so focused on the ministry that he neglects to teach his children to do right. Or it might be discovered that instead of dealing with sin, he attempted to sweep their sin under the rug. In those situations, it's important to know what 1 Timothy 3 teaches and what it does not teach.

If a pastor is doing his best before God to biblically raise a rebellious child and deal with the child's sin, he is meeting the qualification for ruling his house well. I know some preachers whose children struggled, but they loved and encouraged them and eventually saw them come back to God and their families. I remember one specific time when a pastor was going to resign from his church because one of his sons had gone into sin. A wise deacon said to him, "Pastor, if you resign, the rest of us who are struggling with our children won't have an example of how to love them back to God." I'm so thankful that pastor stayed on in the ministry.

If a pastor has failed to train his children or to deal with them when they sin, he has not satisfied the qualification of one that "ruleth well his own house." But if a pastor has done all he can to love, train, and correct his children, his children's actions don't disqualify him from the pastorate. As that wise deacon said, those times present an opportunity for the pastor to show his congregation how to love a child back to God.

CHAPTER SIX

Does God Command That All Giving Be Done in Secret?

Years ago, a preacher accepted an invitation from a church to preach the dedication sermon for their new building. He arrived at the church about ten minutes before the service and was told that the church needed to raise $6,500 by the next day to finish paying for the building. The church officers told him that they were depending on him to raise the money.

After preaching the sermon, the man said, "These men bid me to tell you that you must give $6,500 in cash, which is all due tomorrow. Will you provide it?"

After the preacher's appeal began the slowest, most reluctant offering he had ever witnessed. After 30 minutes they had $3,000—not even half of what they needed. Finally, the preacher said, "What do you expect of me? I am your guest. I do not happen to have the other $3,500. "

A woman stood and addressed her husband who was at the front of the church, recording what was given. With conviction in her voice she said, "Charlie, I have wondered if you would be willing for us to give our little cottage just paid out of debt. We were offered $3,500 in cash for it yesterday. We were told we could get it at the bank any time in ten days, if we chose to make the trade. Let's give our little house to Christ that His house may be free. When we remember, Charlie, that Christ gave His life for us, I wonder if we ought not to give this little house to Him."

Charlie responded in the same spirit, "Jennie, dear, I was thinking of the same thing. We will give $3,500."

Silence reigned for a minute. Then, grown men began sobbing, and almost in a moment that $3,500 was given by men and women who for the last half hour had either refused to give or had given grudgingly.

Many visitors had come for the special service, and before an invitation was given, men and women came down every aisle in the church wanting to be saved.

The gratefulness of that one couple for what the Lord had done for them and their desire to give to Him prompted others to give and many to get saved.

Sadly, the original attitude of the men and women of that church is the attitude of many in our churches today. If someone mentions money in church, we grow uncomfortable, quiet, reluctant, and even rebellious towards the thought of giving. And those who do give faithfully look at their giving as confidential—something they never discuss.

We know that giving is something we're commanded to do, but the bottom line is that it's an uncomfortable topic. To us, how much money we make, spend, and give is deeply personal. Partly because of the sensitivity and partly because of a misinterpretation of Scripture verses, the teaching that no one should ever know what another person gives has come to be commonly accepted. Pastors are advised not to look at giving records, and it is considered a tremendous breach of etiquette for anyone to know how much a person has given. In fact, I've known of people who refuse to use church offering envelopes because they don't want anyone else to know how much they are giving.

But is all this secrecy right? Does God actually command that giving be done secretly?

THE COMMON TEACHING

This concept that God requires giving to always to be done secretly is primarily based on the belief that God condemns those who give for show. Jesus said:

> Take heed that ye do not your alms before men, to be seen of them: otherwise ye have no reward of your

Father which is in heaven. Therefore when thou doest thine alms, do not sound a trumpet before thee, as the hypocrites do in the synagogues and in the streets, that they may have glory of men. Verily I say unto you, They have their reward. But when thou doest alms, let not thy left hand know what thy right hand doeth: That thine alms may be in secret: and thy Father which seeth in secret himself shall reward thee openly.

—MATTHEW 6:1–4

In Bible days, the Pharisees would literally hire someone to sound a trumpet to attract attention when they were going to the temple to give. They were not giving out of a genuine heart to love and serve the Lord, but out of a desire to impress others with their "generosity" and to gain glory for themselves. In this passage, Jesus was teaching against the attitude the Pharisees had toward giving.

The second tenet to this common teaching is that giving should be a private matter. "But when thou doest alms, let not thy left hand know what thy right hand doeth: That thine alms may be in secret."

Years ago, my family was traveling through Kentucky. We stopped for church on a Wednesday night and when we walked in, I noticed that on the end of every aisle there was a pillar with a slot in it that was used for offerings.

I learned that the church believed passing an offering plate violated the Lord's command to give "in secret." I admire the heart of that church to carefully obey God's

Word, but I also believe they had misinterpreted Scripture in the matter of giving.

Giving is an act of obedience, worship, and spiritual growth. It's another way that we grow in grace. Second Corinthians 8 is a powerful passage in which the apostle Paul shares with us the importance of giving. He told the Corinthian church, "Therefore, as ye abound in every thing, in faith, and utterance, and knowledge, and in all diligence, and in your love to us, see that ye abound in this grace also" (2 Corinthians 8:7).

This grace Paul was referring to was giving. He was literally saying, "Christians, just like you're growing in all these great areas, make sure you're growing in your giving as well." Paul, under the inspiration of the Holy Spirit, wasn't looking at giving as a private grace, separate from all aspects of the Christian life.

What if your pastor got up on Sunday morning and preached about loving others? Our first reaction wouldn't be to think, "That's personal—he shouldn't be preaching about that." Nobody has a problem with a sermon urging people to study the Word of God or encourage fellow believers. If we're comfortable with topics like these being preached, why do we grow uncomfortable when giving, another act of obedience, is mentioned? What does the Bible have to say about private giving?

THE CONTRADICTORY TRUTH

Fill in the blank. God looks, not at our outward appearance, but at our _____. If you thought *hearts,* you're exactly right. And understanding that is important to understanding what Scripture teaches about giving.

The Lord condemns both the method and the motive of ostentatious giving. Everything we do goes back to our heart motives. When Jesus condemned those who give "sounding a trumpet" and "to be seen of men," He was preaching against their motive of public recognition. By condemning them, He was showing those around Him the priority of having the right heart. The Lord said, "A good man out of the good treasure of his heart bringeth forth that which is good; and an evil man out of the evil treasure of his heart bringeth forth that which is evil: for of the abundance of the heart his mouth speaketh" (Luke 6:45). A right heart produces the right actions. If our heart is firmly grounded in the truths of God's Word and we're committed to honoring God in all that we do, we'll obey the Lord in our giving.

Money is a tangible thing, and I think we can be tempted to equate the amount that we give with our spirituality. But God doesn't see it this way. He is pleased when a person struggling to make ends meet gives a sacrificial gift out of a heart of love, even if the amount itself is small.

Studies of philanthropy have shown that most of the people who give hundreds of thousands or even millions of dollars don't tithe to a local church. Why is this?

Often, those who give large gifts like the attention they receive. If you just put your tithe in an offering plate, you won't get a building named after you. You won't receive an honorary doctorate. You won't have a plaque in the foyer of the auditorium. It's likely that no one will know about your faithful obedience.

I'm not saying that this is always the case. I know that many godly men and women who have been blessed financially give joyfully, not because they want attention, but because they love the Lord and want to serve Him.

My point is that our hearts need to be right when we give to the Lord, for that is what the Lord is primarily concerned with.

God never commands us not to let others know what we do for Him. Jesus did say, "Take heed that ye do not your alms before men," but in the same message—the Sermon on the Mount—He also commanded public good works. One of the ways that we encourage others to follow the Lord is through our actions. Nowhere in Scripture, taken in the proper context, are we told that we aren't to let others know what we're doing for God.

God commands us to let others see what we do for Him so that He may be glorified. We're to be shining lights in our world for Jesus Christ. "Let your light so shine before men, that they may see your good works, and glorify your Father which is in heaven" (Matthew 5:16). We can't be lights for the world when we don't take action.

To better understand this, look back to the verse we introduced at the beginning of the chapter: "But when thou doest alms, let not thy left hand know what thy right hand doeth: That thine alms may be in secret: and thy Father which seeth in secret himself shall reward thee openly" (Matthew 6:3–4).

Alms don't mean only money; it's actually a Hebrew word for any righteous deed. So when Jesus said in the same sermon, "Don't do things to be seen of men" and later "Shine your light through righteous deeds in the dark world," He wasn't contradicting Himself. His focus was warning against the motivation behind the action. Doing good for the purpose of being seen is the problem—not doing good in public.

One of the hardest tasks we'll face as believers is keeping our motives right. In Acts 5, Annanias and Saphira learned that the hard way. They sold a piece of land and gave part of it to the church. This was commendable, but here's where they went wrong: they represented their gift as the entire purchase price of their property in full view of the church. They craved the approval and praise of men and wanted to be recognized for their generous gift. Ultimately, God killed both of them because of their lie.

Ananias and Saphira were not condemned for announcing their gift or even giving part of the money; they were condemned for lying about how much they had received.

When we encourage public giving, people are provoked to good works. Not long ago, I encouraged a pastor to check the giving records of his people. He was a little surprised because he'd been taught the same thing that I had—giving was a private matter. But I shared that when I reviewed the giving records, I wasn't discouraged. In fact, I was encouraged by how people were giving.

Finally, after looking at what the Bible teaches about giving, he agreed. Later, he told me, "When I announced I was going to start looking at the records, the treasurer came and said the offerings were up 23 percent!" Although it's not right for people to give to be recognized, it is right for them to give. And it's a good thing for a pastor to encourage people to do right.

This concept goes back to accountability. As a pastor, I ask church members if they've been reading their Bible. I call them if they've missed multiple services. I check up on their prayer lives and witnessing. I'm not trying to be nosy; I have to give an account for the members of our church (Hebrews 13:17). God holds me responsible to know what is going on in the lives of the members of the First Baptist Church of Bridgeport.

In Matthew 6, our theme passage, Jesus wasn't making the point that people should never know what you give. The point is that you shouldn't give—or do any other good work—to be seen of men. Every time you sing in the choir, teach a Sunday school class, work on a bus route, witness, or give financially, you make a choice to bring glory to God or to be seen of men.

Paul actually *commended* the members of the church at Corinth for their commitment to give. He told them, "…Your zeal hath provoked very many" (2 Corinthians 9:2). Paul's public acknowledgement of their giving motivated Christians around the world to give. The question is not *what* you do; it's *why* you do it.

Jesus openly observed what people gave. Long before Paul wrote 2 Corinthians, Jesus openly observed what people gave.

> And Jesus sat over against the treasury, and beheld how the people cast money into the treasury: and many that were rich cast in much. And there came a certain poor widow, and she threw in two mites, which make a farthing. And he called unto him his disciples, and saith unto them, Verily I say unto you, That this poor widow hath cast more in, than all they which have cast into the treasury: For all they did cast in of their abundance; but she of her want did cast in all that she had, even all her living.—MARK 12:41–44

In the above story of the widow with two mites, Jesus was watching what people were giving. I'm not saying you should have a chart in the back of the auditorium, recording the member's giving numbers—that would probably encourage improper motives. But if I mention someone's work on a bus route or his Bible study to encourage others, why shouldn't I also be able to mention someone's giving for the same reason?

There are many biblical examples of public giving. Years ago, we had a special giving campaign for a major project at the church, and I went to a pastor friend of mine for advice. He suggested that I hire a consultant and explained, "A consultant will want you to do something that takes you out of your comfort zone. If you're paying them, you'll be more likely to do things that you really need to do to succeed."

I took my friend's advice. One of the things this consultant told me was to have people announce their gifts. My immediate reaction to that was negative because at the time I believed that giving should never be public. In answer to my doubts, he pointed me to 1 Chronicles 29:3–5. This passage describes David's preparation for Solomon to build the temple. David publically told the people what he personally planned to give for the project.

In response to David's example, the people willingly gave to ensure that all of the materials needed for the temple would be in place before the project started (1 Chronicles 29:6–9). After looking at this passage, I took the consultant's advice, and I was amazed at how well our building program went. Knowing that others around you are committed to the cause has a positive effect on morale and behavior.

When Hernando Cortez invaded Mexico in 1519, he had only a few hundred men to face tens of thousands of Aztec warriors. He knew that if his men had the option of quitting and going home, they might take it. So before they began their march inland, he scuttled their ships. From that point on, they were forced to commit to success. Morale and unity were strengthened when each soldier knew his companions were just as committed as he was.

An incident similar to David's in 1 Chronicles happened in Acts 4:34. The church at Jerusalem was undergoing some financial difficulty. Many of those who were converted on the day of Pentecost came to Jerusalem from far away to stay in the city, fellowship, and learn about Jesus at the feet of the disciples.

But since the converts had only originally planned to stay for a few weeks, they quickly ran out of money. In answer to their dilemma, the Jerusalem believers who had land and houses sold them and publicly brought the money and "laid them down at the apostles' feet" (Acts 4:35). This giving was done in front of the whole church without any rebuke or condemnation. The implication of this story is crucial to our study—it was not wrong for these generous Christians to give publicly.

God knows that our giving can provoke others around us to give as well. For example, Paul publicly told the church at Corinth about the giving of the churches at Macedonia. Even out of their deep poverty, they gave liberally and generously (2 Corinthians 8:1–4). Paul's goal wasn't to exalt the generous believers at Macedonia; it was to encourage and inspire the Corinthian church to give as well.

Throughout these pages, I pray that I've encouraged you in your giving. But I want to leave you with a litmus test of sorts to analyze your giving. You see, what we give is just a small part of a bigger issue.

THE TRUTH APPLIED

Find a quiet place to ask yourself the following four questions, and before God, answer them as honestly as possible.

Am I obeying God by giving? The bottom-line motivation for all Christian service is obedience. You might be thinking, "Wait a minute. Didn't Paul command that we give cheerfully?" Yes, but it seems from the context that Paul was speaking of freewill offerings, not the tithe (2 Corinthians 9:1–11).

The Bible doesn't refer to tithing as "giving the tithe." Instead it talks about "paying tithes" and "bringing tithes." The tithe is something we owe to God. It's been said, "The

Lord loves a cheerful giver, but He'll take money from a grouch." Whether it's tithing or giving, it's important to obey whether or not our hearts are right. Slowly, our faithful obedience will turn into a genuine desire. As God prospers us and prompts us, we'll begin to give over and above the tithe.

I've heard people say, "I just don't *feel* like tithing." But truthfully, not paying your tithes and offerings is stealing from God (Malachi 3:8–9). It doesn't matter if you don't feel like it. Try calling the bank and telling them you're not going to make your car payment this month because you don't feel like you can do it cheerfully. It's the same principle with tithing: we need to do our duty and obey whether or not we have a good attitude.

But I encourage you to rise above the bottom line of motivation by obedience to the top line of love. The Bible tells us that the love of Christ constrains us (2 Corinthians 5:14). As you obey, you'll grow out of the motivation of obedience to the motivation of love.

Am I giving out of gratitude? The psalmist asked, "What shall I render unto the Lord for all his benefits toward me?" (Psalm 116:12). He went on to talk about his intention to pay his vows to God in appreciation for all that he had received.

When we think about the magnitude of salvation, it seems foolish to quibble with God over a few dollars in the offering plate. We have so many things for which to be grateful.

A church was having some financial trouble, so the slightly frustrated pastor told the congregation, "Folks, it's not my church. I don't have the money, and I can't pay the bills. If you don't want to keep it going, it won't because I can't do it alone."

Finally, a man broke the silence and said, "I'll give $5,000 in honor of my son who died in the war." Another man nudged his wife and said, "Let's give $10,000 for our son."

She looked confused and said, "But our son didn't die."

The husband responded, "I know. But shouldn't we give more for a son who lived?"

That attitude of gratitude should be our mindset as well.

Am I giving for the glory of God? It's a poor testimony when churches can't pay their bills. As Christians, we represent Christ. It glorifies God when we demonstrate by how we give that we think He is worthy of our money.

Years ago, I read a story in *Reader's Digest* called "Johnny Lingo's Eight Cow Wife." In the culture in which that story was set, a man would pay a certain price for his wife. An average wife would go for one or two cows. A really talented or beautiful wife would go for three or four cows. Johnny Lingo was known as the best trader in the area, so when he offered to pay eight cows for his wife, everyone was amazed.

But the girl he wanted to marry wasn't particularly beautiful. No one thought she had anything special to offer. Yet her stature in the community skyrocketed because of the price her husband paid for her, and no one doubted how important she was to him.

Do people around us wonder why God is worth so much to us? Giving generously is one of the ways that we show the world what Jesus means to us. And when we honor God with our giving, He honors us as well. "Honour the Lord with thy substance, and with the firstfruits of all thine increase: So shall thy barns be filled with plenty, and thy presses shall burst out with new wine" (Proverbs 3:9–10).

Are my gifts an example and encouragement to others? Your giving can impact the giving of others. In 2 Corinthians 8:1, Paul used the Macedonian church's giving to encourage the Corinthians to give. And we should adopt a similar attitude. Many years ago during a stewardship campaign, I announced in church that I was going to give $80 a week. One man told me later that he determined that night that if I could give $80 making less than he did, he could at least give $75 a week. My zeal provoked him to give.

Again, while giving provides us with the opportunity to influence others to do right with their finances, it's important to remember that the motive for giving should never be to draw attention or praise to ourselves. Proper giving brings glory to God, not to us, and when we understand that everything we have is from God and belongs to God (Psalm 24:1), there is no reason for us to glory in our giving. First Corinthians 4:7 says, "For who maketh thee to differ from another? and what hast thou that thou didst not receive? now if thou didst receive it, why dost thou glory, as if thou hadst not received it?"

So biblical, generous giving is an opportunity to invest in God's work with God's money for God's glory, and in turn, we get to reap the rewards of honoring and obeying God! It's a privilege to be part of the work of God—I'm thankful I get to give.

Dr. John R. Rice used to say, "God wants your money, He wants the wallet your money is in, He wants the pants the wallet is in, and He wants the man in the pants. It all belongs to Him."

When we recognize the truth of that statement, our lives will be transformed. Giving is just one of the many graces of the Christian life. And when we recognize giving as a natural outpouring of a heart of love, we'll do what we are created to do—glorify our Creator.

CHAPTER SEVEN

Are Wives Commanded to Love Their Husbands?

If you ask the average person what their top reason for marriage is, you'll get a variety of answers. Some might say "companionship," and others "financial and emotional security," but by far the most common answer you'll get is "love."

But let's consider this answer with another question. Will a marriage *fail* without love? Arranged marriages, which are not founded on love, rarely fall apart. But as we watch the divorce rate of couples who marry primarily for love hover around 50 percent, it makes you wonder what part love plays in a successful marriage.

Ephesians 5:22–25, one of the most referenced passages on marriage, instructs: "Wives, submit yourselves unto your own husbands, as unto the Lord. For the husband is the head of the wife, even as Christ is the head of the church: and he is the saviour of the body. Therefore as the church is subject unto Christ, so let the wives be to their own husbands in every thing. Husbands, love your wives, even as Christ also loved the church, and gave himself for it."

Based on this passage, the two ingredients for a biblical marriage are for the husband to *love* his wife and the wife to *submit* to her husband. But wait a minute. In this passage, a wife is never commanded to love her husband. So *is* love a must in marriage?

It is true that the two basic roles in marriage are for the husband to love his wife and the wife to submit to, not love, her husband. When couples come to me for marriage counseling, I emphasize these two basic commands of love and submission.

When both spouses fulfill their God-given roles, many marital issues are resolved. Because God created men, women, and marriage in the first place, He ordained those commands with a specific purpose. When we look at men and women's most basic needs, we see why.

A woman craves security. She needs to know that her husband is completely committed to her and will take care of her. She needs to know that he'll love her if her weight goes up, down, or stays the same, if her skin is wrinkled or smooth, or if she's having a good day or a bad day. God understood that basic need of women and commanded husbands to love their wives.

Men, on the other hand, don't need security in the same way that women do. We believe (whether or not we're right is up for debate) that if you put us in the middle of a ten-thousand-acre jungle, we'd find our way out. We'd rub two trees together and start a fire. We'd kill an elephant with rocks. We'd eat dirt if we have to. To put it succinctly, we will survive. That's why we never ask for directions—we don't (or think we don't) need them.

A man's basic needs are affirmation and respect. He wants someone to think he's strong, smart, and a great leader. When a wife submits to her husband, she affirms that she trusts his leadership and helps meet that need.

There are some people who believe that because only the husband is commanded to love his wife, it must be optional for a wife to love her husband. During my years of ministry, I've seen this belief negatively impact marriages and families. A clear understanding of what the Bible says about the role of the husband and wife is vital for a strong, thriving marriage.

THE COMMON TEACHING

The Bible sets a high standard for the husband's love—it is to be the same kind of love Christ has for the church (Ephesians 5:25). This love is sacrificial, generous, compassionate, unconditional, and selfless. Since, however,

Ephesians 5 is silent on the matter of wives loving their husbands, some would say that we shouldn't insist that wives need to love their husbands. Arguing from silence, however, is a dangerous way to interpret God's Word.

If a man loves his wife as Christ loves the church, many say her automatic response will be to love her husband back. Herein lies the danger. Women convince themselves that they'll naturally love their husbands if their husbands are fulfilling their biblical role. As a result, they begin to heap high, unattainable expectations on their spouse, assuming that part of his role is to fulfill those desires. And when their husbands, who are human and will make mistakes, don't perfectly fulfill their needs, bitterness develops. They convince themselves that their husbands aren't fulfilling their roles properly, so why should they love them?

But this philosophy couldn't be further from the truth. While Ephesians 5 may be silent on the matter, the Bible does command wives to love their husbands and in the same unconditional way that husbands are commanded to love their wives.

THE CONTRADICTORY TRUTH

Grasping the importance of true, Christ-like love in marriage is essential to a biblical marriage.

Scripture commands the husband and wife to love each other. In Titus 2, Paul, the same human author of Ephesians 5, describes some of the roles for believers in the body of Christ. Look carefully for the command for wives to love their husbands in the passage below:

> The aged women likewise, that they be in behaviour as becometh holiness, not false accusers, not given to much wine, teachers of good things; That they may teach the young women to be sober, to love their husbands, to love their children, To be discreet, chaste, keepers at home, good, obedient to their own husbands, that the word of God be not blasphemed.—Titus 2:3–5

This time, did you notice how the older women in the church are to teach the younger women to love their husbands? That word *teach* is interesting to me. If love were somehow automatic or guaranteed if the husband loves the wife, why would older women need to teach younger women to love their husbands?

I remember speaking to a preacher who believed wives were not commanded to love their husbands. When I mentioned this passage, he responded, "Well, the Bible just says that one time."

Unfortunately, many people take the same approach to the authority of God's Word as the pastor did. The truth is that God only has to say something to us one time for it to be important enough to pay attention to. Even if it's mentioned briefly, He expects us to believe and practice everything in His Word.

If you read through Titus 2, you'll see many commands for men, but, interestingly enough, the command to love their wives *isn't* listed. But just because it's not mentioned here doesn't make Ephesians 5 optional. If the Lord gives a command, even in one small verse, we need to listen. Instead of picking and choosing passages to back up doctrines that sound plausible, we need to be faithful to the whole counsel of God. God's plan for marriage is for *both* the husband and the wife to love each other, and that love is essential.

Men and women are different. For example, when you walk into a store, you'll likely see a few to several aisles of brightly lit shelves selling multiple brands of makeup. But for men? You might find one or two aisles of grooming products and over-priced shaving cream, but that's it.

Beauty products are a staple of nearly every woman's daily routine. When they wake up, they'll look in the mirror and zero in on any perceived flaws. Men, on the other hand, generally have the opposite view of themselves. When they wake up in the morning, they see their perceived strengths. There's a reason the Bible tells us, "No man ever hated his own flesh" (Ephesians 5:29). Men don't disdain their bodies—they tend to be overconfident in their abilities.

Regardless of how different the husband and wife are, there needs to be love between them. Each needs to learn to understand and express his or her appreciation for the other and to love each other unconditionally.

Scripture requires all believers to love one another. Even if God never told women to love their husbands, we still have God's general command to love everyone. First John 4:7 reminds us, "Beloved, let us love one another: for love is of God; and every one that loveth is born of God, and knoweth God." John 13:35 says similarly, "By this shall all men know that ye are my disciples, if ye have love one to another."

As Christians, we've experienced Christ's miraculous, sacrificial love. When we let that reality sink into our hearts, His love will naturally spill out toward others. And God's general command to love others applies to our spouse as well.

Furthermore, a husband's failure to obey God in loving his wife does not negate the wife's responsibility to love and submit to her husband. Our obligations to God are never contingent on another person's obedience to God.

Years ago, a pastor called me for some advice about tithers in his church. "About one-third of our members tithe. The rest give little or nothing," he explained. Based on my experience as a pastor, that didn't surprise me. Then, the pastor asked, "Those people who don't tithe are demanding. They want this, and they want that. They want me to be there when they call me. How do you distinguish between those two groups in your treatment of them?"

I said, "Treat them both the same." The Bible doesn't say the pastor should feed the flock of God…if they tithe. In fact, how are church members going to learn to tithe if they don't have a pastor lovingly teach them? God doesn't excuse our disobedience because someone else failed in his area of responsibility.

One spouse's obedience to God's commands in marriage doesn't guarantee the other spouse's obedience. A husband who loves his wife sacrificially makes it easier for her to love him, but does not guarantee her response. Jesus loves us with a perfect love, but He doesn't force us to respond the way that He desires. He said, "O Jerusalem, Jerusalem, thou that killest the prophets, and stonest them which are sent unto thee, how often would I have gathered thy children together, even as a hen gathereth her chickens under her wings, and ye would not!" (Matthew 23:37). Time and time again, God has extended His love, yet people reject it.

Think about Judas Iscariot. He spent three years knowing what perfect love was like from Jesus, but ultimately betrayed the Lord. Because God has given each of us a free will, there is always the possibility that a husband or wife will choose to do wrong, regardless of what his or her spouse does.

Years ago there was a woman who attended our church who had married a young man she met at a Christian college. He was actively involved in ministry work and well thought of by the leadership.

She didn't know when they married that he struggled with homosexuality. He had been foolishly counseled that marriage would "fix his problem." They were in full-time ministry when his sin problem finally came to light, and eventually, her husband left her.

That young lady was a sweet Christian girl who had done everything she could to be a godly wife, yet her marriage, through no fault of her own, ended tragically.

No matter what your spouse does or does not do, you have an obligation to do right because you alone are responsible to God for your actions. It's wrong to excuse your lack of love on your spouse's real or perceived failure to fulfill his role in marriage.

THE TRUTH APPLIED

If God commands both husbands and wives to love one another, how can Christian couples apply this truth in a way that strengthens their marriages?

Love is primarily a choice, not an emotion. In marriage counseling sessions, I've had a spouse struggling to love the other say to me, "I just can't *feel* that way about my spouse." But statements like those are buying into how our culture defines love. Biblically, love is not an emotion but an action. Although emotions do often *accompany* love, love is a command we are, without exception, to follow.

I think we all can admit we've had experiences with people who were a little tough to love. During college, I stayed for summer school one year. I thought it would be great to have only one roommate instead of three, but the roommate I got was a little, well, eccentric. His strange habits were a good lesson to me in patience, but I have to admit I was thankful when the summer ended.

I wasn't commanded to like him, but I was commanded to love him. The English writer Samuel Johnson said it well: "Kindness is in our power, even when fondness is not." If I love others like God loves me, their likeability doesn't matter. I'll love them because Christ commands it.

While we cannot control the behavior of others, we can influence their behavior. If I didn't believe I could have a part in influencing people to serve God, I wouldn't be in ministry. I've seen God change people from sinners to saints. I've seen people who were bound by sin, living wicked lives, transformed to be happy and free in Christ.

But I myself cannot change people. If I could, that would put me in charge of their lives and take away part of their need for personal accountability. Romans 14:12 clearly states, "So then every one of us shall give account of himself to God." It would not be possible for God to hold us individually accountable if others could force us to behave as they wish because that removes the freedom of choice.

We can help people change, but we can't force them to change. It's not in our power to force someone to do something by our right actions. The fact that a husband loves his wife is not a fail-proof guarantee that she'll love him back. Neither is the idea that when a wife submits to her husband, he'll love her in return. Our job is to influence others to do right through our words and actions. Then, we can leave the outcome to God.

When John Quincy Adams, our sixth president, ran for reelection, he was defeated by Andrew Jackson. Rather than sinking into depression, he returned home and ran for Congress. He served as a representative from Massachusetts, helping to lead the fight in Congress to abolish slavery. Despite his efforts, however, little progress was made.

When asked if he was discouraged, Adams replied, "Duties are ours; results are God's." There is a tremendous peace in leaving the outcome in God's hands rather than taking responsibility for things we cannot control.

When a dogmatic statement unsupported by Scripture is made, check it out carefully. As we've seen throughout this book, errors and commonly believed false teachings gain acceptance because people fail to compare what is being taught to the Word of God. Even if the teachers are widely respected and looked up to, we should not automatically assume that everything they say is true. We shouldn't be critically looking for mistakes they make, but neither should we naively accept everything they teach.

I remember listening to a pastor I respected teach on justice. As I took notes, he said, "If I didn't see a man do wrong or he doesn't admit to it, then I can't honestly know if this man did wrong or not." A red flag came up in my mind. Deuteronomy 19:15 says, "One witness shall not rise up against a man for any iniquity, or for any sin, in any sin that he sinneth: at the mouth of two witnesses, or at the mouth of three witnesses, shall the matter be established." In effect, if two or three witnesses affirm that a man committed a wrongdoing, even though he denies it, the matter can be put to rest. God knew that there needed to be a way to find the truth.

The pastor who was preaching on justice was a wonderful, godly man who helped and encouraged me in many areas of ministry. But in this case, his teaching was not only unsupported by Scripture; it was directly contradicted by it. If I had accepted his teaching without comparing it to the Word of God, I would have believed something untrue.

Another time I heard a preacher say, "There will never be a nationwide revival. We're living in an age of apostasy, and God never sends revival during apostasy." At first glance, that statement sounds logical, but it's not biblical. In fact, if you study revivals in the Word of God, apostasy is not a reason you can't have revival—it is the reason you *need* to have revival.

Israel was far gone from God when they found the book of the Law in the days of Josiah (2 Kings 22:8). God sent revival in that time of apostasy (2 Kings 23). Although the preacher who was speaking about apostasy and revival was a good friend of mine and generally a biblical preacher, he said something that wasn't true.

We need to be like the Bereans. When Paul preached in the city of Berea, those who heard him compared what he said to the Word of God. Acts 17:11 says, "These were more noble than those in Thessalonica, in that they received the word with all readiness of mind, and searched the scriptures daily, whether those things were so."

The word translated *searched* in our English Bible was used in the Greek legal system to describe the gathering of evidence. It indicates a careful study to determine what is true and what is false.

As we close this chapter, I want you to walk away with two things firmly fixed in your mind. First, in every area of our lives, including marriage, we need to be wary of those who make declarative statements without backing it up with clear Scriptural support. Second, God's command for you to love extends to everyone. We don't have an option to selectively pick who we're going to love. And if we're commanded to love everyone around us, how much more important is it that we should love our spouse?

CHAPTER EIGHT

Is It Legalistic to Have Standards?

One of the fastest ways to get defenses rising is to say the word *standards*. Opinions vary widely from clothing standards to music standards to movie standards. It seems like someone has a standard for almost any issue you can think of.

But are standards really necessary? Should we have standards that we encourage others to follow? For example, if you're a Sunday school teacher, a pastor, or a youth worker, should you instruct those you lead to do something or not to do something that the Bible doesn't expressly mention? What about in our personal lives?

Should we have standards? After all, we're under grace, not the law, right?

It boils down to this question: are standards legalistic? A view within popular Christianity has emerged, stating that standards are just another form of legalism. We can't infringe on someone's Christian liberty by telling people not to _____. If something is not expressly stated in Scripture, we don't have a right to make those decision for people.

That's a common view in our churches, and it deserves an answer. To begin, let's unpack what those opposed to standards say.

THE COMMON TEACHING

At first glance, the view that standards aren't necessary seems logical and even right. After all, what right *do* we have to impose our beliefs on someone else? If the Bible doesn't clearly say anything on an issue, what right have we to make that decision? Aren't standards just really an elevated form of someone's opinion? Those who say yes usually present their view with the following ideas:

Christians answer to God and not to man. Is this statement true? Ultimately, yes. We're told in Romans 14:12, "So then every one of us shall give account of himself to God." We are responsible to God for our behavior and must answer to Him (2 Corinthians 5:10). We've even talked in previous chapters about how we are to obey God rather than man. But those against standards take this verse to mean that we have *no* responsibility to man. And, as we'll see later, that is a misapplication of the verse.

Many standards of behavior are not expressly taught in the Bible. Here's your challenge for today. Find the verse that states, "Thou shalt not watch a movie rated PG-13 and above." Next, find the verse, "Thou shalt not listen to rap music," followed by, "Men shall always wear a suit and tie to church, and women must always wear skirts that go no higher than the knee."

Any luck? It's true that you aren't going to find these types of specific applications in Scripture. And many who are against standards say that if we can't find something directly in Scripture, we shouldn't preach against it.

In areas where the Bible isn't clear, Christians have liberty to decide for themselves. God tells us, "Let every man be fully persuaded in his own mind" (Romans 14:5). Not, "Let every man be fully persuaded by his pastor, youth pastor, or another Christian." While it's true that we should believe something because we've studied it out for ourselves, there are those who take these verses to mean, "If it feels good, you have Christian liberty to do it." They believe *liberty* gives us the right to do anything we want to do as long as the Bible doesn't teach specifically against it.

It is wrong for leaders to set standards and guilt people into performance-based acceptance. "To insist on standards," some say, "is to send people on an unnecessary guilt trip. And beyond that, standards are just a form of performance-based acceptance."

It is true that God accepts us because of who He is, not because of what we do. That encompasses the plan of salvation—God loves sinners and sent Jesus to die for us before we were born. We don't work to earn God's love, grace, and forgiveness, nor do we promise Him to follow a set of rules so He'll accept us. We come to Jesus just as we are.

It is equally true, however, that God gives His children instructions of behavior and blesses us as we obey Him in those areas.

We don't keep God's commands for Him to *accept* us. We were accepted at Calvary. But we do follow God so that we have close fellowship with our Father. The good works that we do after salvation aren't a result of our gritted-teeth performance; they are a result of God's grace working through us.

Although God doesn't accept us based on our performance, no matter where you stand on standards, you do believe in the importance of performance in some instances. To illustrate, imagine yourself as a mother or father, giving some last words of advice to your future son-in-law and daughter. You wouldn't say to your future son-in-law, "I love you no matter how you treat my daughter. I'll feel the same whether you hurt her or love her." If your son-in-law hurt your daughter, you would be disturbed by his conduct and would make every effort to see it changed.

We do hold people to a standard of performance, at least sometimes. Some actions are not tolerable, and rightly so.

What does the Bible say about standards?

THE CONTRADICTORY TRUTH

Believing it's wrong to expect a standard of behavior from others sounds good, but it's not biblical. Yes, we have Christian liberty, but biblically that is liberty to live by grace for Jesus Christ.

Christians are to obey God *and* man. One day, we will answer to God. But we also answer to other people. If you zip down the highway at 100 miles per hour, you'll likely encounter a police officer. If you talked too much in class in elementary school, you were called out by your teacher. It's similar in our Christian lives. God has placed people over us to lead us, strengthen us, and encourage us.

People who are against standards take truth (We answer to God) and make it a partial truth (We *only* answer to God). In reality, we do have an obligation to answer to the authorities God has placed over us. In 1 Corinthians 11:1, Paul said, "Be ye followers of me, even as I also am of Christ." Paul wasn't some wild-eyed, foaming-at-the-mouth legalist trying to guilt-trip those who looked up to him. He was a mature believer who loved the Lord, loved others, and wanted people to follow him as he followed Christ.

The Bible teaches the principle of obedience to authority in both secular and spiritual matters. Wives are to submit to their husbands (Colossians 3:18). Children are to obey their parents (Colossians 3:20). Employees are to obey their employers (Colossians 3:22). Christians are to obey civil authorities (Romans 13:1–2).

It's unbiblical to think that we only answer to God, but many Christians buy into this philosophy. I knew of a church secretary who said she wasn't going to do what the pastor told her to do because she worked for God, not him. (I think it's ironic that she still expected to be paid by the church even though she didn't want to follow its leader.)

Throughout Scripture, God's order is for human leaders to guide His people and carry out His program. Unless an authority asks you to do something that's biblically wrong, you're to obey that authority.

Picture in your mind a fifteen-year-old boy who says, "My parents didn't want me to go out with my friends, but I prayed about it and felt God wanted me to go. I may meet somebody I can witness to or somebody who really needs help."

That fifteen-year-old's intentions may have been pure, but his actions and attitude were wrong. His responsibility was to his parents. Likewise, we cannot substitute our emotions or feelings for obedience to the authorities God has placed in our lives. When we live that way, we are not right with God or man.

Liberty is not license to do wrong. Inadvertently or not, it seems that those against standards pick certain verses to support their position while ignoring others. For example, Galatians 5:1 says, "Stand fast therefore in the liberty wherewith Christ hath made us free, and be not entangled again with the yoke of bondage." This verse has become an anthem of those opposed to standards. Because Christ has given us liberty through His Son, we shouldn't be entangled again with the bondage of law-keeping. Without taking that verse in context, it seems like it's saying, "Christians! You have liberty in Christ. Don't listen to another person's opinions and standards."

But then in verse 13 we read: "For, brethren, ye have been called unto liberty; only use not liberty for an occasion to the flesh, but by love serve one another." Did you catch that? We do have liberty in Christ, but it is not to be used as an occasion to the flesh—as an excuse to do whatever feels good to us.

Grace is another word we use alongside liberty. Because we're not under the law but under grace, those against standards insist that we shouldn't preach that Christians ought to live a certain way.

But let's allow Scripture to define *grace*: "For the grace of God that bringeth salvation hath appeared to all men, Teaching us that, denying ungodliness and worldly lusts, we should live soberly, righteously, and godly, in this present world…" (Titus 2:11–12).

Grace teaches us to live, not however we want, but in a holy and godly manner. We are to be a testimony to the world around us. Truly, to use grace as an excuse to live however we want shows that we don't understand what grace is. In fact, Jude talked about men who turn "the grace of our God into lasciviousness" (Jude 4).

Biblical liberty is not liberty to do wrong but liberty to do right. Before you were saved, you were enslaved to sin. No matter what you did, it was your master. The devil may have deceived you into thinking that you had liberty—that you were your own person—yet you were not.

But someone told you about Jesus. When you received Him as your Saviour, He broke your chains of sin and the Holy Spirit took up residence in your life. That Spirit-empowered freedom to do right is what Christian liberty is all about. You now have the liberty and grace to follow God's commands and live a life that is pleasing to Him.

Here is where the opponents of standards go astray. They cite what is true about salvation (it's a free gift, given to us by grace, and not dependent on our performance) and try to apply it to discipleship. God cares greatly about how we live after we're saved, yet many believe that what we do doesn't really matter because we're under grace.

Living right because we have God's grace at work in our hearts is not legalism. Legalism is any attempt at keeping the law *for* salvation. Before salvation, we're dead in our sins. Ephesians 2:5 tells us, "Even when we were dead in sins, hath quickened us together with Christ, (by grace ye are saved;)."

All we can do as helpless sinners is recognize our need for Jesus and turn to Him in simple faith. Salvation is a gift; it's not something we earn through righteous living.

When Paul asked the Galatians, "Having begun in the Spirit, are ye now made perfect in the flesh?" (Galatians 3:3) he was not talking about Christian living. He was talking about eternal security. Some Christians are deceived into thinking that they have to work in the flesh to stay saved. If they sin enough, they lose their salvation. Great peace comes, however, when we realize we don't stay saved through the flesh; Jesus does all the saving *and* keeping.

In order to be saved, you have to "believe on the Lord Jesus Christ" (Acts 16:31). The second you make the heart decision to call on Christ, you are God's child. If you get drunk, commit adultery, lie, steal, or murder somebody, you're still saved.

Reflect on the magnitude of the gospel. We are saved by grace. We can have total confidence that we belong to Jesus, not based on our works, but based on His finished work on the cross. When Jesus cried, "It is finished," all that was necessary for salvation was accomplished. Nothing we can do makes us saved or makes us stay saved. God's grace is truly marvelous.

After we are saved, we are new creatures in Christ (2 Corinthians 5:17). Definite life change comes about when we allow God's grace and love to truly motivate us. To say that liberty and grace means God is okay with us living however we want completely misses the point of real Christianity. In fact, to better understand the importance of standards and convictions, God set the example for us by establishing standards in both the New and Old Testament.

In the Old Testament, the Israelites had many guidelines to follow. Deuteronomy 22:8 says, "When thou buildest a new house, then thou shalt make a battlement for thy roof, that thou bring not blood upon thine house, if any man fall from thence."

A battlement is basically a railing. In Bible times, houses had steps outside the home leading up to a flat roof. In the evenings, people would sit on the roof to enjoy the cool breeze and relax at the end of the day. God told the people to put guardrails around the roof so that others wouldn't fall.

Could you still fall off a roof even with a guardrail? Sure. Could you avoid falling off a roof without a guardrail? Of course.

But God commanded the guardrails be put up to protect the homeowners. This railing is a great picture of a standard. Standards are practical, protective devices to keep us safe. In the verses immediately following, God gave the Israelites further guidelines—or standards—for their behavior.

"Thou shalt not sow thy vineyard with divers seeds" (v. 9).

"Thou shalt not plow with an ox and an ass together" (v. 10).

"Thou shalt not wear a garment of divers sorts, as of woollen and linen together" (v. 11).

When you got up this morning, did you check the tags inside your clothing to make sure they were all the same fabric? While we're still under the moral law God gave the Israelites in the Old Testament, ceremonial law, like the standards listed above, isn't binding on us today. Jesus "blotted out the handwriting of ordinances that was against us" when He died on the cross (Colossians 2:14).

God issued these specific rules to the Israelites alone to teach them the principle of separation. Separation is a big deal to God, starting with Creation. In Genesis 1:4, God divided the light from the darkness. He wanted to impress on the Israelites the importance of separation throughout their day. When they got dressed in the morning, they couldn't put on a garment made of two different fabrics. As they hitched up their team to plow the field, they could not hitch an ox and a donkey in the same harness. While they planted seeds, they could not sow two kinds of seed in the same field. God wants an obvious difference between His people and the world.

The issue wasn't seeds, fabric, or animals—nothing is morally wrong with those things. The issue was the *principle* of separation. Instead of thinking of standards as arbitrary rules to make our lives boring and miserable, think of them as guardrails to help us keep a principle.

Sometimes, however, it seems like standards aren't as cut and dry. For example, imagine you're in a situation where a fellow believer in Christ has a different standard than you do. Perhaps things are getting a little tense because you're convinced something is biblically fine to do, while your Christian brother thinks it's wrong.

The church at Jerusalem could relate to that scenario. The Gentile and Jewish Christians were clashing over standards, and God, through James and the other disciples, gave some instructions that still apply today.

The early church's missionary efforts were in full swing, resulting in many Jewish and Gentile converts. And, although God's plan is for unity among believers, the believers were struggling because their ethnicity and backgrounds were dividing them.

The Jewish converts thought the Gentile converts should obey the law the same way they did. They saw these new Gentile believers committing acts the Jews (heavily influenced by Mosaic law) thought were sinful. As a result, the Jews wanted the church leadership to enforce their rules on the Gentile believers because, in their opinion, the Gentile Christians were a bad influence and an embarrassment.

In the middle of this heated conflict, they turned to James for help. His wise response in Acts 15:19–21 helps us as we deal with standards in our twenty-first century churches.

First, to the Jews he essentially said, "If something violates your conscience, don't do it. But don't force your rules on someone else, either." To the Gentiles, he said, "Do all that you can to keep the peace with your more conservative brothers in Christ."

Those two principles encapsulate the attitude we should have toward standards and other Christians. If something personally violates our conscience, we shouldn't do it. And if we *can* do something in good conscience that another Christian can't, we need not argue about it or ridicule others for having a different standard.

In this New Testament example, James did issue guidelines, or standards, for the Gentile believers. Two were moral issues: abstaining from pollutions of idols and fornication. Two were not moral issues: abstaining from things strangled and from blood. The Gentiles were asked to accommodate their Jewish brethren to keep from causing offense and making others stumble.

The church leaders recognized the need to set a standard to keep peace in the church. Through this story, we realize it is fully appropriate for New Testament Christians like us to have standards in both moral and non-moral matters. Just as importantly, we learn that it is wrong to do something that we know would offend another brother.

I remember learning this principle as a teenager. One of our neighbors was a part-time Zion Wesleyan Holiness preacher. His wife didn't wear jewelry or makeup and never cut her hair. Even in the heat of summer, the men and women only wore long-sleeved shirts. One day, this man invited me to attend a revival service they had. As I was getting ready to leave, I got out a nice pair of slacks and a blue short-sleeved shirt. I didn't think much about it—it was July, and it was *hot*.

My dad walked into my room and asked, "Where are you going?"

I said, "To church with our neighbors."

"Not in that shirt, you're not."

I replied, "But Dad, we don't believe it's wrong to wear short-sleeved shirts."

"They do; and you're going to their church, and you're going as their guest. Go put on a long-sleeved shirt," my dad answered.

There are some things that may not be sinful, but if it offends a brother in Christ, a grace-filled Christian defers to others in order to keep the peace in the body of Christ.

Bible principles cannot be applied in the absence of standards. Whether you'd term it this way or not, to apply a biblical principle requires having a standard. For example, we're told, "In like manner also, that women adorn themselves in modest apparel, with shamefacedness and sobriety; not with broided hair, or gold, or pearls, or costly array" (1 Timothy 2:9).

It's clear that God wants women to be modest—it's a biblical principle. But a principle in isolation has no meaning. To truly follow a principle means applying it, and that comes through standards. You can't follow the principle of modesty without making a mental choice to wear something or not to wear something. The way you follow a principle is through standards.

Consider this from the perspective of traffic laws. When driving, the overriding principle is safety. But what if your mayor got up one day and said, "We're replacing all speed limits with signs that say 'Be safe!' After all, speed limits are just legalistic traffic laws. Forget the arbitrary rules—follow the principle."

To understate it, chaos would reign. You cannot apply the principle of safety without some kind of standards. Someone must take the responsibility to say, "_____ miles per hour is as fast as you can go on this road." Or "You have to stop here when you come to this intersection."

It's likely that you've never seen a speed limit of 27, 54, or 68 miles per hour. Although it might be more scientific to have a speed limit of 25.4 MPH, and it might be safe to drive at 72.2 MPH, speed limits are general standards set forth to create a safe environment, rather than an exact science to be flawlessly executed.

To a certain degree, so are our standards. I can't prove to you from Scripture that a man's hair should be cut above his ears, but I can prove that a man shouldn't have long hair (1 Corinthians 11:14). I can't prove to you from the Bible what the exact length of a woman's skirt should be, but I can prove that a woman is scripturally obligated to be modest (1 Timothy 2:9).

To follow a principle, we have to draw a line somewhere. Just as the church leaders issued standards for the Gentile believers, we need to establish standards for ourselves and be willing to submit to human authorities who set guidelines in gray areas.

God gives human leaders the responsibility to establish standards of behavior. Ephesians 6:1 commands, "Children, obey your parents in the Lord for this is right." You're not going to find a verse that states what time children should be in bed or how much television they should be allowed to watch, but we believe children should obey their parents in these matters. Although Ephesians 6:1 does not say, "Children obey your parents in the Lord as long as their rules conform exactly to your understanding of Scripture and they can cite clear Bible verses that demonstrate the need for every standard," we know that the command for obedience is not based on understanding or agreement. It is absolute. Our children are to obey what we say as human leaders in a position of authority established by God.

The same principle holds true in a church setting. Hebrews 13:17 says, "Obey them that have the rule over you, and submit yourselves: for they watch for your souls, as they that must give account, that they may do it with joy, and not with grief: for that is unprofitable for you."

Biblically, we are to follow the guidance of our spiritual leaders in the church. As a pastor, I can personally share that this is a heavy responsibility. I can't promise you that every standard at First Baptist Church of Bridgeport, Michigan, is exactly what it should be. But I do promise that, to the best of our ability, every standard is established because we're trying to obey the principles of Scripture.

Decisions about standards can be tough. I remember hearing about two music directors who disagreed about each other's song choices. Each had one song he would play that the other wouldn't, and vice versa. Both of these men earned their bachelor's and master's degree from the same college. They both worked in independent Baptist churches. Ultimately, the difference between them was primarily a matter of taste, not right and wrong.

I may get to Heaven and find out that a song I didn't approve for the choir would have been okay. But somewhere, I have to draw a line, and God places that responsibility on me as the pastor. As I set these standards, I'd rather be overly cautious than overly lenient. I don't insist that the people in our church agree with my reasoning and judgment on every decision at home, but I do insist that what we do in our church meets the standards we have put in place.

Safety is found in following the standards of leadership. I've had people say to me, "I don't see what's wrong with doing/wearing/going/listening to _____." And I reply, "I don't see what's wrong with *not* doing/wearing/going/listening to _____." Does it hurt your Christian life and witness to abstain from these things? Does it make you a worse Christian? Following a standard someone you respect in leadership has established won't hinder your walk with God, but going against a standard of leadership might.

We've looked at what the Bible says about standards. And we've alluded to some problems that arise when it comes to setting standards. So let's get practical. How do we set standards for ourselves and react to others who have different standards?

THE TRUTH APPLIED

Standards, as we've learned, are based on principle. Good standards are not legalistic sets of rules with no biblical basis. How, then, do we formulate standards in our hearts?

Years ago, I preached a series on standards answering that question. I didn't spend my time trying to defend my personal standards. I shared a few standards that I had, but my goal wasn't to shove a list of rules down our members' throats. Instead, my goal was to share principles from Scripture that God expects us to follow and encourage the people of our church to formulate standards based on God's Word. I want them to know the reason behind the regulation.

I'd like to share with you the process for formulating standards that I gave my church family.

First, start with a principle. A principle is a Bible truth by which we must live. For example, Psalm 101:3 says, "I will set no wicked thing before mine eyes."

Second, form a conviction. A conviction takes that Bible principle and forms a personal belief. Based on the principle from Psalm 101:3, I've determined that I shouldn't read or view pornography.

Third, create a standard. A standard is a guideline to help you keep that conviction. For example, I've established the standard not to knowingly walk down the grocery store aisle that carries pornographic magazines. This standard isn't in the Bible, but following biblical principles is. And by keeping this standard, I'm establishing guidelines to help me obey Scripture.

Establishing standards is part of growing in grace. Don't feel like you need to sit down and write out fifty-three standards that you're going to implement starting at 8:00 tomorrow morning. But do evaluate where you currently are spiritually. Are there principles and convictions in your life that need some standards to help you follow them? I'd encourage you to spend some time in prayer, asking the Lord to reveal areas in your life that could use some guidelines. Remember, it's not about the rules. It's about a heart to serve, obey, and love Christ.

Show biblical respect towards those whose standards are different from your own. Having standards is important, but how do we respond to others with standards that are perhaps slightly different? First, respect that person's standards. Never make fun of or look down on someone who has differing standards. It's easy to think that anyone with standards lower than ours is a compromiser, or on the flip side to assume that anyone with standards higher than ours is a Pharisee.

But the Bible says this attitude of comparison is foolish. "For we dare not make ourselves of the number, or compare ourselves with some that commend themselves: but they measuring themselves by themselves, and comparing themselves among themselves, are not wise" (2 Corinthians 10:12).

Several years ago, I preached at two churches in neighboring towns. We'll call them Grace Baptist Church and Faith Baptist Church. The pastor of Grace Baptist Church was fed up with Faith Baptist Church's low standards, telling me that Faith allowed mixed swimming activities for the teenagers. I didn't think much about it until I visited Faith Baptist Church to preach. The pastor of Faith complained to me that Grace Baptist Church was compromising with their music standards.

Each of those pastors was convinced that his church was better because of a higher standard over the other in *one* area. The pastors were making mixed swimming and music the basis of spirituality.

Don't make the mistake of assuming you are more spiritual because you have standards higher than another Christian's. That was the flaw in the Pharisee's thinking in Luke 18:11, "The Pharisee stood and prayed thus with himself, God, I thank thee, that I am not as other men are, extortioners, unjust, adulterers, or even as this publican." Talk about an exalted view of yourself! The Pharisee thought that because he kept a list of rules, he was more spiritual than the publican.

On the other hand, don't make the mistake of thinking that someone with standards higher than yours is an object of ridicule. And be careful around those who ridicule another's standards. Standards don't make you godly; they are simply guidelines to help you obey God. Godliness only comes as a result of your relationship with Jesus Christ.

I know some Christians who have several high standards, yet they are unkind, unchristlike, and unhappy. They've turned Christianity into following a list of rules, not deepening a relationship with Jesus Christ. Similarly, if you think that Christianity is solely about following rules, you'll have the same attitude as the unhappy Christians I know.

Does that mean that everyone who has high standards is an unhappy Pharisee? Of course not. A dear friend of mine pastors a church known for its high standards. When he decided to host a Holiness Conference, another well-known Christian leader said rather sarcastically, "Now I have to go there and learn how to be holy." He didn't like the standards of my friend and was critical of how that church operated.

This godly pastor friend of mine has had people attack him with unkind and untrue comments. Somebody made a critical comment about him to me once, and I replied, "They have a great church. They're getting things done for God. People are being saved and the church is growing. Why would I be critical of them for wanting to be holy and trying to do right?"

I know of wonderful Christians who choose to not have a television in their home. I don't think it's a sin to have a television if it's controlled, but I never want to make fun of believers for having stricter standards than I do. In fact, I'd encourage you, if the time is right, to ask people with higher standards than you do why they came to their conclusion. Maybe God will use other believers to teach you something that will help you grow closer to Him.

If your personal standards are higher than those of leadership, follow yours; if the leader's standards are

higher, follow his. There are people in my church who will not go into any establishment where alcohol is served. I'm firmly against drinking, but I don't have that standard in my life. To people with that standard I say, "God bless you and your heart to obey. Don't go to a place that serves liquor." I don't want them to lower their standards, and genuinely admire their heart for God. Others in my church object to buying anything in a church building, including books from a church bookstore. To those people, I say, "Don't buy anything in our bookstore."

I respect people who live by what they believe, even if I disagree with them on a few points. I don't try to change them to make them agree with me on what is ultimately a preferential standard. Don't just be what everybody around you is; be what you believe God wants you to be. God knows you best. He knows your strengths and weaknesses, and if you believe He wants you to set a higher standard for yourself or your family in some area, obey Him.

There is safety in following high standards. I would much prefer to be a little too strict and stay safe than to risk a disaster by trying to push the boundaries of what is acceptable.

Study God's Word to understand biblical principles. Establish standards to help you keep those principles. Then, through God's grace, use your Christian liberty to do what is right.

CHAPTER NINE

Does God Care Only about the Heart?

When we first meet someone, we usually can't help but notice what they're wearing, their speech, or their conduct. Our culture is driven by outward impressions. If you drive down the highway, you'll probably see a billboard advertising the latest weight loss trend. Turn on the television, and you'll see a commercial promoting revolutionary skin care. Visit a bookstore, and you'll see self-help books proclaiming to transform the way people view you and the way you view yourself.

But God doesn't look at the outward appearance like we do. He focuses on our hearts.

A common teaching has arisen, however, that since God looks on the heart of man the outward appearance shouldn't matter to us. After all, 1 Samuel 16:7 says, "But the Lord said unto Samuel, Look not on his countenance, or on the height of his stature; because I have refused him: for the Lord seeth not as man seeth; for man looketh on the outward appearance, but the Lord looketh on the heart."

But is that verse really teaching *we* should only look at the heart?

THE COMMON TEACHING

The Bible clearly states that God does examine the thoughts, motives, and intentions of our hearts. Hebrews 4:12 says, "For the word of God is quick, and powerful, and sharper than any twoedged sword, piercing even to the dividing asunder of soul and spirit, and of the joints and marrow, and is a discerner [revealer] of the thoughts and intents of the heart."

In our Heavenly Father's omniscience, He sees and knows everything, even what is hidden to us. The psalmist said, "O Lord, thou hast searched me, and known me. Thou knowest my downsitting and mine uprising, thou understandest my thought afar off" (Psalm 139:1–2).

Sometimes, we can feel like people don't understand us. Yet God knows us better than we know ourselves. He is constantly evaluating what's going on beneath the surface of our hearts. He clearly and instantly sees the emotions, feelings, and struggles reaching to the corners of our hearts, and He is always accurate in His assessment of us.

But how many times have we thought that someone was one way when in reality they were completely different? That outward appearance can be a good *indicator* to us as humans of what is going on in someone's life, but it's not fail-proof. We don't have the ability to unequivocally determine what someone's heart looks like.

For example, a well-known evangelist came to our church years ago and preached in chapel at our Christian school. He thought one of our students was making fun of him while he was preaching. After the service, he told me, "That girl has been looking at me scornfully during this entire sermon." When I found out who she was, I was surprised because we'd never had any trouble with her.

The next day, the preacher said it happened again. It was really starting to get to him. He told me that if she made faces the third day, he was going to call her down publicly. Again, I was confused. That girl was a model student, and I'd never seen a negative spirit reflected on her face. Finally, I went to the girl and asked what was going on. Surprised, she told me that she didn't have a problem with this man at all—he had just misinterpreted her expressions.

Our heart is extremely important. Outward appearance can be deceiving, but the heart never is—it reveals who we are. Proverbs 4:23 says, "Keep thy heart with all diligence; for out of it are the issues of life." God expects and commands that we keep Him first place in our hearts (Matthew 22:37).

But here is where a potential viewpoint arises that goes against Scripture. If God emphasizes the heart over the outward appearance, then the outward appearance must be irrelevant or at least unimportant, right?

As we already alluded to, we judge people based on their appearance, but the outward appearance can be deceiving. Sometimes, someone can have a godly heart, but his appearance doesn't exactly look the Christian part. An example is one of the men on my church staff. Years ago when he first got saved, he had long hair. He loved the Lord and had a wonderful heart for Him, but like all of us, he still had some growing to do. Eight months after his salvation, he cut his hair. The change in his appearance signaled a change in his spiritual maturity, not in his heart toward God. It would have been wrong for me to look at him with his long hair and think, "Oh, that man obviously doesn't love the Lord."

I've known people whose dress standards were different than mine, but they were wonderful Christians who loved God and faithfully brought others to Christ. On the flip side, I've known those with very conservative dress standards who were mean, judgmental, and didn't display any of the fruits of the Spirit in their lives.

Just because people don't look the way we think they should look doesn't give us the right to think they are not right with God. What a tragedy it would be to refuse people based on their failure to meet our standards. A church needs to be a place where people feel safe to learn how to grow spiritually. The last thing they need is a condemning eye and a judgmental look from a Christian who has been saved for decades.

God deals with His children at different times about different things. If someone who doesn't look like your suit-and-tie-Sunday-morning Christian comes to your church, welcome them and say, "We're glad you're here. God bless you." We don't have to *approve* of their appearance to *accept* them.

However, the belief that only the heart matters and the outward appearance is completely irrelevant may not be in line with what Scripture has to say about the matter.

THE CONTRADICTORY TRUTH

The Bible is clear about how God looks at our heart and our outward appearance. While the heart is certainly *more* important, the outward appearance matters too. Both work hand in hand as we grow in our Christian lives.

Above everything else, we need to be right on the inside. Why are we commanded to guard our hearts? Why such a heavy emphasis on what no one can even see? Heart change produces lifestyle changes. Our outward appearance will slowly be affected by our inward heart, but never the other way around. One of the reasons the member at my church cut his hair was because God was working in his heart. Because his heart was right with the Lord, his obedience demonstrated on the outside.

Sooner or later, a wrong heart will manifest itself outwardly. I've had people sit in my office after badly losing their temper and excuse themselves by saying, "Well, I'm not really like that. I was just under pressure that day." Times of intense pressure can cause us to react worse than we normally would. The reason that bad attitudes emerge when we're under pressure, however, is that they were inside in the first place. If you squeeze an orange, grape juice doesn't leak out. You get orange juice because that is what's inside an orange.

Dr. Bob Jones, Sr. used to say, "Behind every tragedy of human character is a long process of wicked thinking." All of us will have a wrong thought or attitude enter our minds—often many times a day. When that happens, we have a choice to either get rid of that thought or allow it to linger. If we allow it to linger, our behavior will eventually follow. And this is a key reason why God wants our hearts to be right toward Him.

Having our hearts right will produce an incredible outward transformation. But that doesn't mean that we should just "let the outward take care of itself." On the contrary, God does want us to be right on the outside.

Repeatedly, God gave standards for the outward appearance. In the Pentateuch, God gave the Israelites several specific instructions concerning what He wanted them to wear. Even today, you'll see this observed by many Orthodox Jews who wear something called a *tallit*. On the *tallit* are fringes called *tzizit*. This comes directly from Numbers 15.

> And the Lord spake unto Moses, saying, Speak unto the children of Israel, and bid them that they make them fringes in the borders of their garments throughout their generations, and that they put upon the fringe of the borders a ribband of blue: And it shall be unto you for a fringe, that ye may look upon it, and remember all the commandments of the Lord, and do them ; and that ye seek not after your own heart and your own eyes, after which ye use to go a whoring: That ye may remember, and do all my commandments, and be holy unto your God. I am the Lord your God, which brought you out of the land of Egypt, to be your God: I am the Lord your God.—NUMBERS 15:37–41

God wanted visible reminders of His commandments on the Israelites' clothes. Remember, this commandment was given to the nation of Israel as part of ceremonial law to govern their behavior. Although it's not binding on us today, the principle illustrated by this commandment is for us. Our outward appearance does matter to God.

If God only cared about the heart, why would He instruct men to have short hair, for example? First Corinthians 11:14 says, "Doth not even nature itself teach you, that, if a man have long hair, it is a shame unto him?" Clearly, God wants there to be a difference between men and women. Gender distinction is, in part, an issue of outward appearance.

Our church has leadership requirements for outward appearance. My desire isn't to be unnecessarily strict, but I still want to err on the side of caution. For example, men and women who serve in our ministry have certain dress code requirements. We ask that they not go certain places in town that could damage their testimony. One day, I may learn that I was a little too strict or even a little too lenient in some areas, but my heart isn't to impose a bunch of preferential standards. I simply want to obey the Lord.

You might be thinking, "Wait a minute. What about 1 Samuel 16:7? God literally told Samuel not to judge David based on his outward appearance. After all, David was a young, short, sunburned shepherd. In Samuel's eyes, he probably didn't look like king material, but God saw David's heart."

At first glance, you're right. The verse says, "But the Lord said unto Samuel, Look not on his countenance, or on the height of his stature; because I have refused him: for the Lord seeth not as man seeth; for man looketh on the outward appearance, but the Lord looketh on the heart" (1 Samuel 16:7).

Taken in the context most assume for this verse, Samuel was judging David on his less-than-kingly appearance, and God was warning against that. But God wasn't telling Samuel not to judge David, He was telling Samuel not to judge Eliab, Daniel's older brother. God knew that Samuel's natural inclination would be to gravitate toward Eliab because he looked like a ruler. When we grasp the true context of this verse, we realize that 1 Samuel 16:7 isn't saying, "Don't judge someone who looks bad on the outside because he might have a good heart." It's actually saying, "Be careful about judging someone who looks good on the outside because his heart may not be good."

Ultimately, what only God saw in Eliab's heart in 1 Samuel 16 was revealed to everyone in 1 Samuel 17. When Goliath issued his infamous challenge against the Israelites and the God of the Israelites, David, who wasn't even in the Israelite army like Eliab, was the only one strong enough to stand against the giant's taunts. Instead of encouraging his younger brother, Eliab criticized David and accused him of having wrong motives for going against Goliath. While Eliab may have looked the part, God knew his heart wasn't right.

God chose to use David, not because of what he looked like, but because of his heart. David's love for the Lord was clearly revealed in every interaction and conversation throughout 1 Samuel 16 and 17. David honored God, was obedient to his father, had faith in God, and stood up for what was right. When falsely accused, he didn't respond in anger but focused on doing what God wanted. It was because of David's genuine desire to serve God with his heart that God used him.

THE TRUTH APPLIED

Our outward appearance is so much more than the clothes that we wear. In fact, our outward appearance reveals much about us.

The outside appearance is a revelation. Often, we can tell how someone feels about us just by how they look at us. Genesis 31:2 says, "And Jacob beheld the countenance of Laban, and, behold, it was not toward him as before." Laban's face revealed that his heart had changed toward Jacob. Laban didn't need to say a word for Jacob to understand that things weren't as before.

I remember something similar happened to me with a sweet family in our church. One Sunday, I could sense tension between this family and me. They avoided eye contact, the husband wouldn't shake my hand, and they barely said hello when I greeted them. I immediately wondered if I had done something to upset them.

Finally, I learned that they had gotten one of our staff members a Bible for his birthday. When he opened the package, he said, "I knew you were going to give me this Bible." They asked how he knew, and he told them I had informed him what his present would be. He was kidding with them—I knew nothing about the gift—but they took his teasing seriously. They were upset with me because they thought I had ruined their surprise, and their inward displeasure showed on their faces and in their outward behavior.

Our face is often an indicator of our feelings toward someone or something in our hearts. In fact, it seems like our face can be like a billboard advertising the very real feelings we have in our hearts.

The outside appearance is a reflection. Our outward expression shows who the master of our heart is. Exodus 34:29 says, "And it came to pass, when Moses came down from mount Sinai with the two tables of testimony in Moses' hand, when he came down from the mount, that Moses wist not that the skin of his face shone while he talked with him." Moses' face shone because he had literally been in the presence of God.

The same thing happened to Stephen in the New Testament. When he was brought to trial before the Sanhedrin, "all that sat in the council looking steadfastly on him, saw his face as it had been the face of an angel" (Acts 6:15).

The outward aspects of our lives—the way we dress, talk, and behave—reflect our inward relationship with God. When our heart is right with God, our actions will naturally follow. Our face will reflect the joy of the Lord. And it won't be something we have to artificially drum up. Moses didn't even know his face was shining, and he wasn't trying to impress people. He had just been with Jesus, and it showed in his countenance. Likewise, our countenance should show if we've been with Jesus.

We should strive for balance in both our inward and outward appearance. It's important to believe and teach what God's Word says about outward appearance. But, even as we do so, we should be careful of the trap of the Pharisees. Look at what Jesus said:

> Woe unto you, scribes and Pharisees, hypocrites! for ye make clean the outside of the cup and of the platter, but within they are full of extortion and excess. Thou blind Pharisee, cleanse first that which is within the cup and platter, that the outside of them may be clean also. Woe unto you, scribes and Pharisees, hypocrites! for ye are like unto whited sepulchres, which indeed appear beautiful outward, but are within full of dead men's bones, and of all uncleanness. Even so ye also outwardly appear righteous unto men, but within ye are full of hypocrisy and iniquity.—MATTHEW 23:25–28

The Pharisees were convinced that as long as everything looked good on the outside, things were fine. But no amount of outward compliance with rules can ever substitute for obedience in the heart.

In Psalm 51:6, David said, "Behold, thou desirest truth in the inward parts: and in the hidden part thou shalt make me to know wisdom." The sin of the Pharisees was hypocrisy. On the outside, they were model Jews who stringently kept the law. But on the inside, they were far from the Lord.

It's important to find the right balance. We should emphasize the outward appearance along with the inward appearance. In a sense, the two are inseparable, for the right heart leads to an outside change. But, while we emphasize the outward appearance, we should never forget that the heart is more important. We shouldn't get caught up in a list of standards while forgetting about our heart. Nor should we look down on others who don't believe the same way that we do. We're told in Romans 14:4, "Who art thou that judgest another man's servant? to his own master he standeth or falleth. Yea, he shall be holden up: for God is able to make him stand."

Make it your goal and purpose to be right both on the inside and on the outside. Since God looks on the heart, I need to have a right heart to please Him. Since man looks on the outward appearance, I need to have a good testimony in my appearance to draw men to God.

I heard about a young girl who volunteered to help her mom with the dishes. As her mom watched, she saw that her daughter was washing only the inside of the cups. When asked why, the little girl said, "Well, the pastor said he'd rather have things clean on the inside!"

If I had to choose between a clean outside or a clean inside, I'd pick a clean inside. Yet it's far better to have the dishes clean inside *and* out! In our walk with God, we do not have to choose between inward and outward righteousness. He calls us to honor Him in both.

CHAPTER TEN

Was Jesus Born on December 25?

Walk into any major store in early November and you'll likely see red and green, ornaments, candy canes, and cheerful signs wishing you a Merry Christmas. Christmas music may play gently in the background. But you know that this is just a preview of what's coming.

The day after Thanksgiving, Christmas fever will descend in epidemic proportions. The mad dash will be on to find the perfect Christmas gift. Homes will be overtaken by twinkling Christmas lights, waving blow-up snowmen, and holiday parties complete with eggnog and peppermint hot chocolate. Airports will be packed as people travel home for the holidays. And, in the hustle and bustle, it's easy to lose sight of why we're celebrating.

Most of us have heard sayings such as, "Jesus is the reason for the season," or "Keep Christ in Christmas," or "Wise men still seek Him." All of these are true. We celebrate Christmas as the time when Jesus came to earth as a baby to redeem us.

But some Christians question the origin of Christmas. Perhaps their greatest concern is that the holiday, quite possibly, originated out of a pagan celebration. (In fact, in the early days of the Massachusetts Bay Colony, a fine of five shillings was imposed on anyone found following the "popish tradition" of celebrating Christmas.) Also, it's impossible to dogmatically say that Jesus was born on December 25. Finally, Christmas has lost much of its earlier meaning of celebrating Christ's birth and degenerated into a holiday focused on the "spirit" of the season and Santa Claus.

These are fair objections, and we're going to take a closer look together. Celebrating or not celebrating Christmas isn't a doctrine, and I certainly wouldn't end friendships over it, but I also don't think it's something we need to be confused about. In fact, in my study of the holiday's origin, I was encouraged by an aspect of the Bible's reliability that we'll consider at the end of this chapter.

THE COMMON TEACHING

Under the reign of men like Nero and Diocletian, Christians suffered immense persecution. Still, the government was unable to stifle their faith as these believers continued to boldly take a stand for Christ. All of that changed, however, in AD 313. The Edict of Milan was passed under Constantine, legalizing Christianity. Many say that it was around this time that Christmas as we know it originated.

Some oppose Christmas because of its apparent pagan origins. In the fourth century, the Roman emperor Constantine was facing a large battle against significant odds. He claimed he had a vision and saw a cross. A voice said, "In the sign of the cross conquer." Assured of victory, he won the battle.

As a result, he made Christianity a legal religion in the empire. "Christianity," in this sense, is an all-encompassing term, including not just biblical Christianity but also false religions that claimed the same name but were really a combination of pagan practices with Christian terms.

Historians contest the sincerity of Constantine's conversion, but he certainly made an impact throughout his empire. People began converting in huge numbers in an effort to conform to the new, in-vogue religion. Since the pagan priests in their temples were now facing unemployment, they simply added a few rituals, changed a few names, and called themselves Christians. These priests gave Christian names to pagan practices, and, heavily influenced by the pagan culture, Roman Catholicism began to form. In pagan religions, we see an idea of a divine mother with her child. Roman Catholicism took this concept and applied it to Mary and Jesus. It's possible this pagan culture began worshipping Mary as a substitute for their gods and goddesses.

One of the pagan elements that supposedly slipped into Christianity during the Roman Empire was Christmas. Some say it came from the celebration of Mithra, the Persian god of light. In AD 274, years before Constantine, Aurelian instituted the celebration of Mithra's feast every year on December 25. When Constantine made Christianity legal, worship of Mithra was widespread, especially in the Roman army. As a result, the Roman Catholic Church took the pagan Zoroastrian holiday and renamed it Christ's Mass.

Interestingly enough, however, early Christian sources had *already claimed* December 25 as the date of Christ's birth. It wasn't a date that came to be just because of a pagan holiday. For example, Sextus Julius Africanus, according to the Encyclopedia Britannica, identified December 25 as the date of Christ's birth in AD 221. Also, many commentaries by Hippolytus, an early Roman commentator who lived years before Aurelian, give December 25 as the date. According to the *International Book of Christmas Carols*, Telesphorus instituted public church services to celebrate the nativity around AD 130. At the same time, Theophilus was urging the celebrating of Christ's birth on December 25. All of these predate Aurelian's decree to celebrate Mithra on that day. Given Aurelian's animosity to Christianity, perhaps *he* was the one trying to take over a holiday!

An alternate view of the Roman origin of Christmas was that it was intended to replace the celebration of Saturnalia. But I would question this as that celebration ran from December 17 to December 23. It seems that if Christmas had been instituted as a replacement, the Romans would have extended the celebration through the 25th.

What we do know, however, is that the first recorded celebration of Christmas on December 25 in the Roman Empire occurred in AD 333, twenty-five years after Christianity became the state-sponsored religion. To be fair, I do think we can say Christmas, at least to some extent, was influenced by pagan elements. I do not think, however, we can say that Christmas was *started* by pagan Romans. Nevertheless, this pagan association has led many Christians to frown on the celebration of Christmas.

Others oppose Christmas because Christmas trees appear to be forbidden in Scripture. Jeremiah 10 seems to be describing a Christmas tree: "For the customs of the people are vain: for one cutteth a tree out of the forest, the work of the hands of the workman, with the axe. They deck it with silver and with gold; they fasten it with nails and with hammers, that it move not" (Jeremiah 10:3–4).

But this passage doesn't refer to our custom of putting up and decorating Christmas trees. The verses surrounding it are clearly talking about idols made from trees. Jeremiah was explaining that since idols cannot speak or move and have no power, there is no need to be afraid of them (Jeremiah 10:5).

Furthermore, there is sufficient historical evidence to contend that the Christmas tree has a Christian origin. Dr. John R. Rice explains that, in the eighth century, a missionary named Boniface went to Germany to preach Christ. The Germanic tribes worshiped the oak tree as a symbol of deity, but Boniface told them the oak tree was a poor symbol for God. It sheds its leaves and appeared to die each winter. The tree that should remind them of God, he said, was the evergreen for it is always green and thriving.

That German influence spread. Christmas trees became popular in England primarily through the influence of the German-born Prince Albert, husband of England's Queen Victoria. In America, they were introduced by the German immigrants to Pennsylvania. Contrary to what is sometimes believed, the Christmas tree has a Christian origin and isn't forbidden in Scripture. I think it can be an enjoyable and memorable part of celebrating Christ's birth.

Some oppose Christmas because of its materialistic pull. More and more, Christmas moves away from its focus on Christ's birth. Even Christians can easily get wrapped up in how the world approaches the holiday. For example, while I don't think that Santa Claus is wrong, I do think we should be careful about presenting him as truth to our children. If we lie to them about Santa Claus, they might be tempted to wonder if we've lied to them about other things.

(And honestly, I didn't want some fictional stranger getting the credit when I was the one spending all the money on Christmas gifts for my kids.)

Along with the idea of Santa Claus, we can fall into the trap of excessive materialism. The push to buy, buy, buy from Black Friday to New Year's Day can be overwhelming, and we can miss what Christmas is all about. When we keep things in the proper perspective, however, I think it's wonderful that we have a special day set aside to celebrate the birth of Christ.

THE CONTRADICTORY TRUTH

The big question we posed at the beginning of the chapter—was Jesus really born on December 25?—is one we can answer reasonably. Based on our study of Scripture, I do think there are legitimate grounds to say that Jesus was born on or very near to that day. Of course, we can't read between the lines in the Old Testament prophecies and determine that Jesus was actually born on December 25. Yet if we take a closer look at Scripture, we can establish that it was *possible* for Jesus to have been born close to the traditional date. Let's look at a few clues:

The Jewish religious year begins with the month Nisan. The Hebrew calendar has 354 days instead of 365, so their calendar does not exactly line up with the one we use. The Hebrew month Nisan roughly corresponds with mid-March to mid-April on our calendar, and it's in this month they celebrate the Passover and Israel's deliverance from Egypt.

The priests who served in the temple served after a pattern established by King David. According to 1 Chronicles 24, the descendants of Aaron were divided by David into twenty-four groups to serve two roles—governors of the sanctuary and governors of the house of God (1 Chronicles 24:5). Each group of priests served according to a schedule drawn up by the casting of lots (1 Chronicles 24:7–18).

It would seem from 2 Chronicles 23:8 that the priests served for a week at a time. This meant that each group knew when they were due to leave their homes and go to Jerusalem for their time of service. Each would serve twice a year, along with the mandatory feasts of Passover, Firstfruits, and Tabernacles, when all the priests served. These feasts would complete the entire year in their calendar.

Zacharias, the father of John the Baptist, served in the eighth course. Luke 1:5 says, "There was in the days of Herod, the king of Judaea, a certain priest named Zacharias, *of the course of Abia*: and his wife was of the daughters of Aaron, and her name was Elisabeth." According to 1 Chronicles 24:10, the family of Abijah was assigned the eighth course. That meant that Abijah and his descendants after him would fulfill their duty to serve in the eighth and thirty-second turns. Because of how the feasts fell, this would be the ninth and thirty-fifth weeks of the year.

As a descendant of Abijah, Zacharias would have served in the temple in these two weeks of the Hebrew calendar. They would fall in the spring and autumn on our calendar. Zacharias was fulfilling his normal term of service when the angel Gabriel appeared and told him he and Elisabeth were going to have a son.

If this was the second rotation for the year, Zacharias would have completed his service and gone home in the fall. The Bible tells us that Zacharias stayed and completed his normal duties in the temple before returning home (Luke 1:23). It was probably shortly after Zacharias' return home in the fall that Elisabeth conceived, as promised by the angel. The date for the conception of John the Baptist in this case would be the end of October. Elisabeth hid herself five months after conceiving John (verse 24).

Gabriel appeared to Mary in the sixth month of Elisabeth's pregnancy to announce the birth of Christ. The start of the sixth month of Elisabeth's pregnancy would have probably been early spring. At this time, Gabriel announced to Mary that she would be the mother of the Messiah and that her cousin Elisabeth was expecting (Luke 1:26–36).

Normal gestation for a human baby is nine months. If the angel Gabriel made his announcement to Mary sometime in the early spring, she would have reached full-term, nine months later, sometime in winter. We don't know for certain that Jesus was born on December 25, but a careful study of Scripture gives us good reason to believe that it could have been close to that date.

Remember the shepherds the angels appeared to? If Jesus were born on December 25, they were outside, watching their flock on a cold winter night, which doesn't seem to be the norm.

I believe the field between Bethlehem and Jerusalem may very well have been the location of the "tower of the flock," mentioned in Micah 4:8. In this field, shepherds kept the spotless lambs chosen for temple sacrifice all year round. Since the verse comes just seven verses before the great Messianic prophecy of Christ's birth in Micah 5:2, it's quite possible this was a prophecy of where the announcement was to be made, and that these special shepherds were the ones who heard the angels.

Although some Christians may object to celebrating Christmas, it's not legitimate to do so on the basis that Jesus couldn't have been born at that time. Christians have been claiming December 25 as the date from early on. Scriptural chronology lines up with that date. Alfred Edersheim, the famous author of *The Life and Times of Jesus the Messiah*, stated, "There is no adequate reason for questioning the historical accuracy of [December 25]. The objections generally made rest on grounds, which seem to be historically untenable."

THE TRUTH APPLIED

You may wonder why we're spending a chapter debating the exact day Jesus was born. Isn't it enough to simply remember Christ's birth? It's true that picking a time to purposefully meditate on Christ's birth is more important than nailing the right date. But studying the timeline of Christ's birth also helps us to recognize an amazing truth.

As I studied Christmas in light of Scripture, an exciting truth was renewed in my mind as I saw the accuracy of God's Word related to the historic study of when Christ was born. The Bible is a never-ending resource of truth, growth, and transformation. It is always worthy of study and incredibly trustworthy.

Let's take a closer look at the power of Scripture.

The Bible adds up—every time. Every time I find an answer in the Bible, I'm reminded afresh that I can take what the Bible gives me and always arrive at a logical conclusion. It's encouraging to know that the Christians were celebrating December 25 for centuries, but if we didn't have that information, we'd still have the shepherds in the fields with their Passover lambs and the calendar calculations from Zacharias to establish winter as the time of year Christ was born.

God has given us a wonderful, living Book. We could study the Bible for the rest of our lives and never run out of things to learn.

If you have a question about how something in the Bible could be true, the answer isn't to automatically assume that the Bible is wrong. Patiently and attentively study Scripture. The Bible has always been proven right and the skeptics proven wrong.

For example, some used to criticize the Bible because there was no evidence of the people called the Hittites who were spoken of in the Old Testament. Through the years, the archaeologists continued digging. Ultimately, they found ample proof of the existence of the Hittites. The skeptics do everything they can to shake our faith and cast doubt on God's Word. But ultimately, God's Word always prevails.

The Bible has more to tell us than we have learned. Have you ever thought, "I've been in church my whole life and read the Bible every day for years. What more could the Bible teach me?" I think many of us have been guilty of thinking that, at least for a moment.

A man once told me, "I've been in church so long that I've heard every sermon there is to preach."

I replied, "Truthfully, sir, I haven't even heard all of my sermons yet."

Whether you've been saved three days, three years, or three decades, the Bible always has something new for us. I've been saved for years and read the New Testament every two months and the Old Testament every three months. I don't discover deep and wonderful truths every day, but as I seek the Lord's face when I read His Word, He often speaks to my current needs and teaches me something new.

I remember once preaching a sermon about Phinehas, Aaron's grandson, who stopped a plague by killing the Israelite who brought a Midianite woman into his tent (Number 25:6–8). In passing, I mentioned that later on in his life Phinehas made it to the Promised Land (Joshua 22:13). Someone came up to me after church and said that he must have been under twenty because all the men twenty years old and up died in the wilderness except Caleb and Joshua.

His question got me thinking. I read more carefully and found that the death penalty pronounced on all the men twenty years and older did not apply to the Levites. They were not counted when the people were numbered (Numbers 26:62–63). All of the Levites could go to the Promised Land, regardless of their age. That nugget of truth had been there the entire time; I just hadn't noticed it before.

The Bible is worthy of our consistent reading and studying. Do you have a time and place for studying God's Word daily? We can get so wrapped up in the responsibilities of our lives that we push off reading God's Word throughout the day. By the time our day ends, we might squeeze in a few verses, whisper a brief prayer, and resolve to do better the next day.

But God is worthy of so much more than that. If you don't already, determine to set aside a time and place to read the Bible. Ask God to speak to your heart and show you the special truths He has for you. If you come to a portion of Scripture that you don't understand, ask God for wisdom to study it for yourself. As you explore the Bible, you will continue to find transforming truths.

As I studied the birth of Christ, Galatians 4:4–5 kept running through my mind, "But when the fulness of the time was come, God sent forth his Son, made of a woman, made under the law, To redeem them that were under the law, that we might receive the adoption of sons."

"When the fullness of the time was come…" is a powerful phrase. I wish we had time to fully develop what this historically means, but I'll mention one aspect especially fascinating to me. The Lamb of God who came to take away the sins of the world (John 1:29) was born at the same time the lambs out in the field were being born. The shepherds visited by the angels in Bethlehem, just a few miles from Jerusalem, quite possibly could have been the same shepherds who kept the sheep for the temple to provide the lambs for the sacrifices. That's incredible symbolism! The shepherds literally came face-to-face with angels announcing the birth of the Messiah who would fulfill the law and abolish the need for those sacrifices.

We can always count on God to work at exactly the right time in exactly the right way. God has perfect timing, both in the birth of His Son and in our lives as well. Carefully studying God's Word shows us how God makes "every thing beautiful in his time" (Ecclesiastes 3:11). And when we seek out God's Word, we'll discover treasure greater than even what the best gold miner can find.

CHAPTER ELEVEN

May We Defend Ourselves, or Must We Always Turn the Other Cheek?

One night, a burglar decided to rob a Quaker's home. Knowing that Quakers are pacifists, he thought the house would be an easy mark. When the Quaker was startled awake by the intruder's noise downstairs, he grabbed his hunting gun and cautiously moved toward the living room.

Catching the intruder quietly unloading a drawer of valuables downstairs, the Quaker aimed his gun directly at the man. "Friend," he said, "I mean thee no harm, but thou standest where I am about to shoot."

That old story holds a relevant question. What *does* the Bible say about self-defense and responding to opposition?

It seems that many religious groups, such as the Quakers and the Amish, strongly hold the principle of pacifism. Shunning any form of self-defense or war, they back up their beliefs using verses such as Matthew 5:39 where Jesus said, "But I say unto you, That ye resist not evil: but whosoever shall smite thee on thy right cheek, turn to him the other also."

I've found that, out of a heart to obey God and out of confusion over a few Bible passages, some Christians refuse to defend themselves or join the military. Perhaps an even more common assumption is that Christians should not respond to any criticism. But is Matthew 5:39 correctly interpreted to mean we should never fight back? Should we defend ourselves against unjust criticism?

THE COMMON TEACHING

Clearly, Jesus did command that we turn the other cheek in Matthew 5:39. And in the events leading up to and during His crucifixion, He refused to fight back or defend Himself.

The incredible restraint that Jesus showed during this time is a powerful testimony. Jesus literally spoke the world into existence. He raised the dead, healed the blind, and fed thousands of people with just a few pieces of bread and fish. To defend Himself against those arresting Him would have been as easy as speaking a word. In fact, Jesus said, "Thinkest thou that I cannot now pray to my Father, and he shall presently give me more than twelve legions of angels?" (Matthew 26:53).

Jesus didn't fight back. Instead, He went to the cross "...as a lamb to the slaughter, and as a sheep before her shearers is dumb, so he openeth not his mouth" (Isaiah 53:7). Pilate noticed His silence in the face of the accusers and said, "Answerest thou nothing? behold how many things they witness against thee. But Jesus yet answered nothing; so that Pilate marveled" (Mark 15:3–5).

Jesus remained silent, not because He was powerless, but because He specifically came to earth and "gave himself a ransom" (1 Timothy 2:6) for our sin.

Because Jesus showed such restraint, it seems that we should also do the same by not defending ourselves, going to war, or standing up for ourselves when we're falsely attacked physically or by critics.

Before we close the case on self-defense, however, let's look at a few other passages in the Bible. What does the Bible teach about answering opposition?

THE CONTRADICTORY TRUTH

The night before the crucifixion was hardly the first time Jesus faced attack. Hostility toward His teaching was a regular occurrence during His ministry on earth. For example, at one point the Pharisees came to His disciples, demanding an explanation for why their Master ate with sinners.

> And it came to pass, as Jesus sat at meat in the house, behold, many publicans and sinners came and sat down with him and his disciples. And when the Pharisees saw it, they said unto his disciples, Why eateth your Master with publicans and sinners? But when Jesus heard that, he said unto them, They that be whole need not a physician, but they that are sick. But go ye and learn what that meaneth, I will have mercy, and not sacrifice: for I am not come to call the righteous, but sinners to repentance.—MATTHEW 9:10–13

When the Pharisees criticized Jesus for spending time with sinners, He didn't let their criticism go unanswered. The Pharisees were questioning Jesus' very purpose in coming to Earth—to seek and to save sinners. Through this story and others, we see a balanced approach. Here, Jesus *did* respond to criticism. Yet other times, such as during His arrest and crucifixion, He did not.

All of us are going to face attacks for what we believe. And, in the heat of the moment, it can be tough to have the restraint to respond biblically, not emotionally. Let's look at a few principles concerning what Jesus said about self-defense.

We need to protect our testimony. If we're living for God and standing for what is right, people are going to attack us. This is where determining the right response can get difficult. Many would say that, under all circumstances, we should just let criticism, attacks, and opposition go.

One well-known, respected preacher told me that he never responds to criticism or defends himself. Another man I knew said, "Never explain and never complain."

It's true that sometimes the wisest choice is to step back and let God step in. In some circumstances, God wants to completely take care of the matter for us without our involvement, but the Bible also says, "A good name is rather to be chosen than great riches" (Proverbs 22:1). That verse is powerful. Our good name—our testimony—is more important than *great* riches. If we have a good name, it doesn't matter what our financial state is—we have a priceless possession.

What do people think when they hear *your* name? Encouraging? Negative? Joyful? Compassionate? Uncaring? Diligent? Lazy? The impression people have of us is vitally important—so much so that we need to confront and correct attacks that could potentially damage our good name.

One time, a preacher I knew gave an interview for an article. Among other things, he said, "The way to keep from changing your convictions is to keep associating with the same people. I know a man who used to associate with a certain preacher, and now he doesn't. He's changed." Although he didn't give names, he described circumstances so similar to mine that I had a hunch the negative comments he made were directed toward me. (Over the years, I've found that the people who criticize you to others are usually embarrassed to confront you directly. They don't seem to mind talking *about* you, but they wouldn't dream of talking *to* you.)

I called him to ask if he had been referring to me. When he admitted that he was, I said, "You're my friend, and I respect your opinion. As far as I know, I've remained true to my convictions. I still use the same Bible, and I still share the gospel with others. I haven't lowered the standards at our church. But if there's an area I need to strengthen, I want you to show me. I don't want to compromise my beliefs."

He answered, "You don't go to such-and-such meetings anymore. You don't preach for so-and-so anymore."

I replied, "That's true, but you were talking about changing convictions. Mine are still the same, even though I don't associate with that man any longer. He changed his beliefs; I didn't think that in good conscience I could speak for him or continue going to his meetings."

The man sincerely apologized and told me he'd choose his words more carefully in the future. My heart wasn't to attack or bully this man but to protect my testimony. If a critic or even a well-meaning Christian questions something in your life that could potentially damage your good name, it's your duty to respond to it.

Our good name is one of the greatest treasures that we have, and we must actively seek to build it. Shakespeare recognized this, eloquently describing its importance in *Othello*:

Good name in man and woman, dear my lord,
Is the immediate jewel of their souls:
Who steals my purse steals trash; 'tis something, nothing;
'Twas mine, 'tis his and has been slave to thousands;
But he that filches from me and my good name
Robs me of that which not enriches him
And makes me poor indeed.

If someone robs our home, we can replace what they've taken. But if someone steals our reputation from us, we've lost a great treasure. A good reputation is often impossible to regain. Protecting our good name isn't just limited to defending yourself when someone attacks you. Far more than that, it means building up your reputation *before* the attacks come. Are your day-to-day actions above reproach? Are your thoughts and words kind and edifying, not slanderous? When attacks and criticisms come, it's easier to defend yourself if you've already established a godly pattern of living in your life.

Jesus instructed the disciples to prepare to defend themselves. Jesus didn't look at self-defense as somehow unspiritual or fleshly. In fact, He not only defended himself, he specifically instructed His disciples to arm themselves *for* self-defense.

Then said he unto them, But now, he that hath a purse, let him take it, and likewise his scrip: and he that hath no sword, let him sell his garment, and buy one. For

> I say unto you, that this that is written must yet be accomplished in me, And he was reckoned among the transgressors: for the things concerning me have an end. And they said, Lord, behold, here are two swords. And he said unto them, It is enough.—LUKE 22:36–38

The Lord placed such a high level of importance on protection that He told the disciples to sell their garments to buy a sword if necessary. In Bible times, people didn't own many changes of clothing, and every clothing article they had was valuable. By giving such drastic instructions, Jesus was emphasizing the importance of protecting yourself.

God commanded His people to go to war. Although the decision to go to war needs to be made with utmost care and deliberation, at times it may be the only solution to fully defending ourselves and our country. Think about the Israelites. They constantly went to war over their enemies—at God's command.

> Samuel also said unto Saul, The Lord sent me to anoint thee to be king over his people, over Israel: now therefore hearken thou unto the voice of the words of the Lord. Thus saith the Lord of hosts, I remember that which Amalek did to Israel, how he laid wait for him in the way, when he came up from Egypt. Now go and smite Amalek, and utterly destroy all that they have, and spare them not; but slay both man and woman, infant and suckling, ox and sheep, camel and ass.
> —1 SAMUEL 15:1–3

We cannot read the Bible honestly and conclude that God always disapproved of war for any reason. Unless you misinterpret Scripture passages like the one above, pacifism is not taught in Scripture. In fact, in the war God commanded against the Amalekites, the Israelites were not defending themselves against attack—it was an offensive, retributive war. God was judging Amalek for what they had done in the past by commanding His people to execute the utter destruction of the Amalekites.

Jesus made distinction between the right cheek and the left. Every word of the Bible is important. Instead of saying, "If someone smite thee on thy cheek," Jesus added a word. He said, "If someone smite thee on thy *right* cheek." If the aim of this verse was simply to say, "Christians, if someone attacks you, either physically or verbally, turn the other cheek to them," why wouldn't He just say "cheek" or "right or left cheek"?

Jesus was deliberately making a distinction. Between 85 and 90 percent of people are right handed. A right-handed person facing someone would slap the left cheek, not the right cheek. If two people were standing facing each other, the only way for one of them to smite the right cheek of the other would be with the back of the hand.

Many cultures, including Jewish, taught that it was a double insult to strike someone with the back of the hand rather than with the palm. I remember a story Dr. Bill Rice told of meeting a group of seven warriors on his missionary trip to Africa. What he did not know until later was that those men had just killed a group of Dutch workers. As they approached him, the leader tried to stab Dr. Rice with his spear, but it caught on his belt buckle. Dr. Rice reacted by slapping him with the back of his hand, and, to his surprise, the warriors immediately retreated.

He later said his quick response must have been God protecting him. In tribal culture, a chief rebuked a warrior with a backhand slap. When the warriors saw Dr. Rice respond similarly, they assumed he was a great leader.

When Jesus said, "Turn the other cheek," He was explaining that you do not need to respond to every insult thrown your way. He was not, however, telling the disciples to not defend themselves against physical attack.

If you are attacked, you have every right to defend yourself. In fact, you have an obligation to defend your family from physical danger. As we saw previously, Jesus told the disciples to buy a sword to defend themselves.

Self-defense was so important to our American Founding Fathers that they included the Second Amendment in our Constitution. We have the right to keep and bear arms to defend ourselves, our property, and the people around us. It's true that sometimes we shouldn't respond to attacks and criticism. But to completely step away from our God-given and Constitutionally-protected right to defend ourselves is not only dangerous, it is unbiblical.

At this point, you might be wondering, "But what about when I am criticized? Is there a right way and a wrong way to respond?" That's a valid question. If we don't have guidelines in place for how and when to respond, we could potentially do great damage to the cause of Christ.

THE TRUTH APPLIED

When you're faced with opposition, there are a few vitally important questions to ask. Having a biblical foundation helps to ward off many problems that could arise when you're in the heat of the moment.

Am I protecting myself or others around me from a genuinely dangerous, physical attack? Of course, if someone is rushing toward you with a knife, please don't stop to contemplate, "Is this really dangerous?" Nothing in the Bible, properly interpreted, teaches against defending yourself and those around you from physical attack. If someone attempts to harm me or someone I love, I'm going to fight in self-defense.

But sometimes, if we're not in imminent danger, we can choose not to retaliate. For example, the pastor of a church where I used to serve was making visits when the man he was visiting punched him in the face. Instead of saying anything or fighting back, the pastor just left the house. This man went around bragging about how he'd beaten up the pastor. Someone heard him talking and said,

"That man is a Golden Gloves boxing champion. He could have knocked you out cold. He just chose not to!"

In this case, the pastor knew that retaliation could have harmed the cause of Christ. His goal was to lead this man to the Lord, not start a fist fight that would eliminate his chances to reach the man with the gospel.

If you're in genuine danger, protect yourself. But if you're not, ask yourself if responding would do more harm than good to the cause of Christ. If the answer is yes, make the choice to walk away.

Will a response to this attack genuinely help? If you're making an impact in the world, people are going to attack and criticize you. Many of those attacks, snide comments, and unfounded criticisms aren't worthy of a response. But other times, if someone attacks your character or falsely accuses you of some moral failing, it's both right and appropriate for you to respond. As we saw earlier, Jesus did this with the Pharisees. Although He did not attack them in return, He did explain the true motives for His behavior.

Questions and criticisms generally come from two different categories of people. First, there is a group that genuinely cares about the truth. Responding to them is a powerful response to lies and accusations. But other people are just looking for the next rumor to spread. Answering them rarely helps because they are so fixated on spreading lies.

Pray for discernment as you decide what the best course of action is. Will a response genuinely help in your situation? Or will simply ignoring the attack help the fire die down faster?

Am I fighting back out of a fleshly motive or desire for revenge? Nowhere in the Bible are we told, "Thou shalt get even with thy neighbor." As you look at your motives, ask yourself, "Am I trying to protect my good name or myself from bodily harm? Or am I just seeking retribution?"

Vengeance belongs to God (Romans 12:19). No matter what happens, you never have the right to take justice on yourself. Sometimes, God wants you to take action. Other times, He wants you to step back and let Him take care of it. Determining what your motives are and listening to the Holy Spirit's leading will help you determine what to do next.

It is essential to learn the discipline and power of restraint. Criticism and false attacks are difficult. But they can help us grow in our faith. For one, they help us to learn the grace of restraint.

When Jesus said to turn the other cheek, He was encouraging His disciples to exercise restraint. If we're insulted, our natural response is to fight back. We don't like what was said about us, and we're determined to let the person that hurt us know what he did.

When those times come, it is vital that we ask the Lord for grace under pressure. This takes much more willpower than fighting back does, but the results are incredibly worth it. We will have learned discipline, protected the cause of Christ, and diffused a potentially volatile situation.

We need to know the difference between what we should respond to and what we should just let go. For example, I think more Christians should grow upset over the cause of Christ being harmed. But too often, I see people more upset over an insult that hurt their pride or discouraged them. Their focus was on themselves, not on how they could advance the cause of Christ.

I remember hearing about a man who was a member of our church in its early stages, years before I was pastor. The church was officially organized in 1952, and the charter members completed their first building in 1963. In fact, that little building still stands today. From what I've read in the records of the church, the church started meeting there before the heating system was hooked up. People brought in charcoal grills to warm up the building.

Most of the work on the building was done by the members. During the first service, the pastor stood up to thank people who had worked on the project. There was one man, a builder by trade, who had done more than anyone else to get the building done. And his name was the only name the preacher forgot to call out. That man said, "That's it. I did all that work and put in all that time. The pastor doesn't appreciate what I did, and I'm never going back to his church again." As far as I know, he kept his word. The sad truth was that this man wasn't injured—just insulted.

It's easy to grow angry when we're falsely attacked. In the heat of the moment, we may try to defend ourselves, but quickly lose control. Even if we were innocent of what was said about us, we can damage our testimony with just a few angry words and actions.

Have you ever seen someone argue with such great intensity about something so trivial that you've gotten embarrassed for them? You inwardly cringe as they grow angrier. You realize that person's attempt at defending himself is doing more harm than good. Or maybe you yourself have been in a similar situation. It's so easy to let our emotions master a situation. Instead of responding with grace, we get angry and hit back at the person who attacked.

Situations like this were what Jesus was referring to when He said, "Turn the other cheek." He wasn't saying, "Don't defend yourself," or deal with a matter that puts a mark on your character. He meant that if people insult you, you don't need to respond. Instead, you can choose to let it go. God is a just God. He'll never let a false attack go unpunished. You can rest confidently in a God who has the power to always take care of your problems.

CHAPTER TWELVE

Is There a Difference Between Big Sins and Little Sins?

I heard about a man who was once called to serve on a jury. The case under consideration involved a marijuana possession charge. The defense attorney, in questioning the prospective jurors, asked this man whether he made a distinction between large offenses and small offenses. The man replied, "I believe that if you borrow a penny, you're in debt." Immediately, he was excused from serving on the jury. To have a chance at winning the case, this lawyer needed someone who believed in differences between big and small offenses.

Ever since I can remember, I've heard people insist, "There are no big or little sins with God. It's all equal in

His eyes." I believe many people readily accept this idea because they don't want to minimize a "small" sin. But when we take a closer look at what the Bible says, this concept is actually a misinterpretation of Scripture. Even in our desire to encourage others to do right, it's important that our viewpoint is aligned with Scripture.

THE COMMON TEACHING

Those who believe the Bible does not make any distinction between big sins and little sins point to the fact that God's Word condemns sin broadly. It's true that we're not going to find a verse that says adultery is worse than lying. But it's also true that, as we study God's Word, we find that God does place weightier consequences on some sins over others.

One verse those who believe sin is equal in God's eyes point to is Matthew 5:21–22. Jesus said, "Ye have heard that it was said of them of old time, Thou shalt not kill; and whosoever shall kill shall be in danger of the judgment: But I say unto you, That whosoever is angry with his brother without a cause shall be in danger of the judgment: and whosoever shall say to his brother, Raca, shall be in danger of the council: but whosoever shall say, Thou fool, shall be in danger of hell fire." They believe that in this passage, Jesus was saying to be angry was equal with murder. They also point to James 2:10, which states, "For whosoever shall keep the whole law, and yet offend in one point, he is guilty of all."

We mentioned earlier that some emphasize that God views all sin equally because they don't want to treat any sin lightly. But we can also go to the other extreme of this belief. Once, a man told me, "My looking at pornography is no worse than someone else's judgmental attitude." He used the idea that all sin was the same to justify significant sin that was wrecking his life.

Another time, I counseled a man who was upset because his church would not allow him to teach Sunday school or be a deacon because he smoked. He rationalized, "Everyone sins. My sin is just in my pocket." He didn't see why that one visible sin should keep him from holding a leadership position in the church.

It's easy—but dangerous—to justify sin by pointing out the faults of others. Yet this philosophy is coming up in Christian circles everywhere. Satan knows that he may not be able to tempt you with an obvious, glaring sin. But if he can convince you that what you're doing isn't really wrong because perhaps it's "not as bad as so-and-so's sin," he has won half the battle.

In Psalm 19:12–13, however, the psalmist emphasized just how detrimental the smallest sin can be in our lives: "Who can understand his errors? cleanse thou me from secret faults. Keep back thy servant also from presumptuous sins; let them not have dominion over me:

then shall I be upright, and I shall be innocent from the great transgression." The psalmist, under the inspiration of the Holy Spirit, understood that there were sinful areas in his life he didn't know about. He desperately wanted God to reveal those areas to him. Like the psalmist, we need to ask the Lord to reveal those blind spots in our lives.

Although saved by grace, Christians are imperfect people. For example, G. Campbell Morgan, the famous Bible commentator, drank brandy. Charles Spurgeon, the prince of preachers, smoked cigars. D. L. Moody, a famous preacher of the late twentieth century, was so overweight that he would literally rest his stomach on the pulpit while he preached. But no matter how hard you look, you aren't going to find drinking, gluttony, or smoking condoned in the Bible. In our desire to follow Christians that have a strong walk with God, we still need to stick to the Bible.

A musician friend of mine told of a famous conductor he once studied under. The man was frustrated that his students weren't grasping the important lessons he was trying to teach. Finally, he said, "How I talk and how I spit—this they copy." We need to incorporate the virtues, not the flaws or even the inconsequential attributes, of great Christians.

When we start to think that any sin is okay if we can find another godly Christian that does it, we become a combination of the worst traits of the strongest Christians. It's never permissible to deny the Lord like Peter did, to commit adultery and murder like David did, or to kill a man in anger like Moses did. Were these men great Bible characters? Yes, absolutely. Does that give us justification to do whatever they did? Absolutely not. We should be modeling our lives based on the unchanging truth of God's Word. If a Christian we respect deviates from a biblical command, we must stick to the Bible.

THE CONTRADICTORY TRUTH

Sin is what separates us from God. It's why Jesus had to go to the cross and the reason for suffering, death, and sickness in our world.

But what if we peel back the layers? As we asked at the beginning of the chapter, does God distinguish between adultery and a white lie, for example? Does God look at some sins as worse, so to speak, than others? To find out, let's look at a few biblical concepts.

There are no acceptable sins. Our world constantly makes judgments about what is acceptable and what is not. For example, if you robbed a bank and were caught, the arresting officer wouldn't let you free with just a slap on the wrist. But if you drove seventy in a sixty-five miles-per-hour zone, it's likely you'd be let off with a warning or not even be pulled over at all. We constantly make judgments about what is excusable and what is not.

That's not the case with God. God never looks at a sin and says, "Oh, don't worry about that. It's no big deal."

James 2:10 tells us, "For whosoever shall keep the whole law, and yet offend in one point, he is guilty of all." If we break even one of God's laws, we're just as guilty before God as if we'd broken all of them.

Think of the Ten Commandments as ten links in a chain. You as a lost sinner are suspended over Hell by that chain. To fall, how many links do you have to break? Only one. Once you have broken the law, you are a lawbreaker. And once you're a lawbreaker, God, who is just, cannot let you into Heaven. James was emphasizing that no matter which sins you have committed, if you've committed *any*, you're in trouble with God.

Does that mean we should throw our hands up in the air and think, "Well, I disobeyed my parents when I was four—I might as well commit adultery when I'm forty"? Or "I've already lied to my boss; I might as well steal money from him too"? Of course not. When the grace of God takes root in our lives, we'll begin to understand just how incredible salvation is. Because God has forgiven us— because we've been declared *not guilty*—we should seek to live in a way that pleases the Lord.

We must understand that even the smallest sin grieves and displeases the Lord. Psalm 66:18 says, "If I regard iniquity in my heart, the Lord will not hear me." If we knowingly harbor sin in our lives, our relationship with God will be severely impacted.

My friend Dr. Curtis Hutson had a niece who was killed in a car accident. He told me that a few years later, at a family gathering, he and his relatives were watching old home movies that had his niece in them. After a few moments, his brother and sister-in-law slipped outside.

Dr. Hutson followed them and saw them crying on the front porch. When he apologized for bringing up painful memories, his brother told him, "Don't be sorry; it just hurts so much." As Dr. Hutson walked back inside, he told me that he thought of the verse, "Grieve not the holy Spirit of God" (Ephesians 4:30). He said, "It struck me that I can do something that makes God feel even more grief than my brother and sister-in-law felt over the loss of their daughter." When we sin, it hurts the heart of God.

Different sins have different consequences. Yes, all sin is a big deal to God, and all sin grieves Him. But not all sin has the same consequences. Look back to Mosaic Law, for example.

> For it is the life of all flesh; the blood of it is for the life thereof: therefore I said unto the children of Israel, Ye shall eat the blood of no manner of flesh: for the life of all flesh is the blood thereof: whosoever eateth it shall be cut off. And every soul that eateth that which died of itself, or that which was torn with beasts, whether it be one of your own country, or a stranger, he shall both wash his clothes, and bathe himself in water, and be unclean until the even: then shall he be clean.
> —LEVITICUS 17:14–15

These two verses make a distinction between a person eating the blood of an animal that he killed and eating something that died on its own. For eating the blood of an animal he killed, a person was cut off; for eating something that died a natural death, he was simply unclean.

Years after Moses wrote Leviticus, Solomon wrote about this same concept in Proverbs.

> Men do not despise a thief, if he steal to satisfy his soul when he is hungry; But if he be found, he shall restore sevenfold; he shall give all the substance of his house. But whoso committeth adultery with a woman lacketh understanding: he that doeth it destroyeth his own soul. A wound and dishonour shall he get; and his reproach shall not be wiped away. For jealousy is the rage of a man: therefore he will not spare in the day of vengeance. He will not regard any ransom; neither will he rest content, though thou givest many gifts.
> —PROVERBS 6:30–35

In Bible times, a thief was to repay four or seven times what he stole (depending on the item stolen)—a stiff penalty to be sure. But the penalty for adultery was destruction of the soul. What a contrast! God can forgive adultery, but it is the only sin in the Bible that God says never loses its reproach.

There is no sin that is excusable, and there is no sin that God will not forgive. Yet some sins have greater consequences than others.

Earlier, we mentioned Psalm 19:12–13, the passage that spoke of secret faults. These verses state, "Who can understand his errors? cleanse thou me from secret faults. Keep back thy servant also from presumptuous sins; let them not have dominion over me: then shall I be upright, and I shall be innocent from the great transgression" (Psalm 19:12–13).

Did you catch the distinction between presumptuous sins and secret faults? According to this passage, some sins are considered to be larger transgressions than others. Secret faults are sins we commit that we don't know about. Presumptuous sins, however, are sins that we knowingly choose to commit. And when we purposefully sin, that sin gains dominion over us. We start out the master, but we end up the slave.

Although there are no good, acceptable, or irrelevant sins, some sins do have greater consequences than others. As Psalm 19 tells us, presumptuous sins lead to the greater transgression. When we know something is wrong but think we can handle it, we're entering dangerous ground. The Bible says, "Wherefore let him that thinketh he standeth take heed lest he fall" (1 Corinthians 10:12). No sin is tame enough for us to handle.

THE TRUTH APPLIED

George Orwell was a famous writer on social issues in the first half of the twentieth century. His classic parable on

Communism, *Animal Farm*, told the story of animals who ran the oppressive farmer off and took over the operation of the farm themselves. At the beginning of their rule, they posted several guiding principles on the side of the barn. The first principle stated, "All animals are equal."

Over the course of the story, the pigs rise to a leadership position at the farm and begin living off the work of the other animals. As time passes, they changed the rules to benefit themselves. Finally, the first principle is rewritten to read, "All animals are equal, but some animals are more equal than others."

Those pigs could tell the other animals that everyone was equal, but the truth was, they weren't. Likewise, we can try to convince ourselves that all sin is equal, but the truth is, some sins are *not* equal.

Driving 150 miles per hour and double parking are both against the law. But which ticket will be worth more? Speeding at 150 miles per hour is worse than double parking and thus will have more serious consequences.

All sin is wrong. Even if we tell one lie, we're guilty of all. But some sins are worse than others, and ignoring that truth is dangerous because it opens the door to rationalizing our sin.

Never excuse your sin by comparing it to the sin of another. When I was a young preacher, an older pastor and I started talking about preachers and temptations they face in ministry. He mentioned, "You hear about these guys messing up and committing adultery. For every one who commits adultery, ten compromise; and for every ten who compromise, one hundred are proud. The compromising and proud preachers do far more harm to the cause of Christ than one preacher who commits adultery. Remember, David was called a man after God's own heart before and after his sin."

But this pastor's statement wasn't true. As we've already seen, the Bible clearly teaches that adultery has greater consequences than other sins. In fact, the Bible specifically mentions that David's adultery brought great reproach to the Lord (2 Samuel 12:14).

Years later, I learned that the same preacher had been involved in an immoral relationship. Although I can't see his heart, I have to wonder if he was trying to downplay his own sin. I remember that he would sometimes imply that we ought to sin so we can experience God's grace. But the apostle Paul said, "What shall we say then? Shall we continue in sin, that grace may abound? God forbid. How shall we, that are dead to sin, live any longer therein?" (Romans 6:1–2). This man failed to recognize that the Christian with a heart to follow God is concerned with living for the Lord and repenting of sin—that's what God's grace teaches us to do. I believe that this man's wrong view of sin was a major part of his downfall. Likewise, when we minimize sin because a person we respect is doing it or we can point to someone else doing something "just as bad," we're an easy mark for the devil.

Live a life that pleases the Lord. For many years, the greatest animal trainer in the world was Gunther Gebel-Williams. He was so outstanding that the Ringling Brother and Barnum and Bailey Circus purchased the entire European circus company for which he worked so they could add him to their show.

Gebel-Williams was known as the "Lord of the Rings," and his flamboyant smile never faltered whether he was working with horses, elephants, tigers, or lions. His amazing act was the highlight of the circus for more than twenty years.

In an interview not long before he retired, Gebel-Williams revealed the reason for his quitting the circus. He said that, in part, he was too accustomed to the big cats that were the centerpiece of his act. He felt that he had lost some of his fear of them—and realized how dangerous this was.

Gebel-Williams realized that the lions weren't something to trifle with. Likewise, we need to realize that sin is never something to be trifled with. The devil, just like that lion, is actively seeking opportunities to devour us and destroy our lives. This is why 1 Peter 5:8 warns, "Be sober, be vigilant; because your adversary the devil, as a roaring lion, walketh about, seeking whom he may devour."

It's important to your spiritual health and your relationship with God that you maintain the proper attitude toward sin. Don't excuse a sin because someone you respect allows it. Don't tolerate anything remaining in your life that you know to be wrong. Remember, the devil is actively seeking to destroy you. Only as you remain committed to following God, no matter what the world around you does, can you live a life that is pleasing to the Lord.

CONCLUSION

It takes dedication, perseverance, and courage to challenge assumptions and go against the status quo. In these pages, we've covered topics from Christmas to burnout to giving in secret. But, as you may realize, those are just small parts of the much bigger picture—God's truth is incredibly important. The most seemingly insignificant assumption we believe can drastically impact our life. It can transform our marriage, change our giving habits, or alter our approach to criticism—for better or worse.

I hope that these pages have inspired and challenged you in two ways. First, I pray that you've been challenged with the great care we need to take in approaching

Scripture. Too many times, we can take someone's words, a blog post we read, or a book by a Christian author, and accept it as truth. Or perhaps we read a verse, take it at face value, and develop a "truth" that gets popularized over time. We shouldn't be critical, looking for faults, but we should be diligent students of God's Word as we filter what we hear.

Second, I pray that you'll consider what assumptions you may have held. Study Scripture, and go to God's Word as your final authority. The closer we draw to the Lord and His truth, the more fulfilled, blessed, and happy we will be.

Ultimately, I pray that you will be better equipped to, not only challenge assumptions, but also to live out the truths of God's Word.

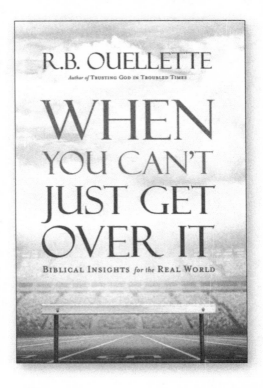

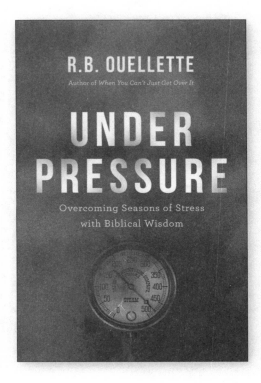

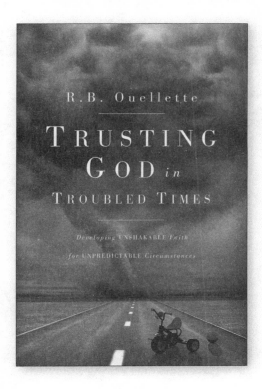

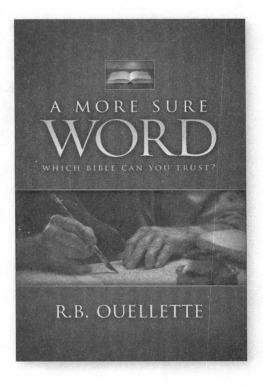

BOOKS WE THINK YOU WILL LOVE...

Trust and Obey
365 Devotions to Encourage Your Walk of Faith

Paul Chappell's Trust and Obey devotional will encourage your spiritual growth. The readings conclude with a solid takeaway principle which you can apply to your life immediately. You'll be challenged and encouraged to follow Jesus more closely and to walk with Him in practical ways throughout each day.

Are We There Yet?
Marriage—The Perfect Journey for Imperfect Couples

This book is for every couple at any stage of the marriage journey. It will help reveal a God-given perspective that can change and strengthen your marriage. A companion guide is sold separately.

Making Home Work in a Broken Society
Bible Principles for Raising Children and Building Families

God has entrusted you, as a parent, to care for and raise your children for Him—but it's not easy. Discover what it means to invest in your children and how you can bring them up in the nurture and admonition of the Lord.

STRIVINGTOGETHER.COM
ALSO AVAILABLE AS EBOOKS